SOUNDING BOARDS

SOUNDING BOARDS

Advisory Councils in Higher Education

BY MICHAEL J. WORTH

Sounding Boards
Advisory Councils in Higher Education

Copyright ©2008 by Association of Governing Boards of Universities and Colleges,
1133 20th Street, N.W., Suite 300, Washington, D.C. 20036

Printed and bound in the United States of America.

Library of Congress Cataloging-in-Publication Data

Worth, Michael J.

Sounding boards : advisory councils in higher education / by Michael J. Worth.

    p. cm.

Includes bibliographical references and index.

    ISBN 978-0-9792425-0-2

    1. Universities and colleges—United States—Administration. 2. School management and organization—United States—Decision making. 3. Advisory boards—United States. 4. Educational surveys—United States. I. Title.

LB2341.W655 2008

378.1'01—dc22

        2008012101

Cover photography: "Piano Strings 2," by Matt Billings

SOUNDING BOARDS
Advisory Councils in Higher Education

FOREWORD VII

PREFACE IX

CHAPTERS 1

    Boards in Higher Education 1

    Purposes and Roles of Advisory Boards and Councils 15

    Organizing and Managing Advisory Boards and Councils 29

    Working With the Advisory Board or Council 41

    The Bottom Line: Costs and Benefits 49

APPENDICES 57

    Sample Advisory Council Bylaws and Guidelines 57

    Cases

        Whittier College, *Poet Council* 65

        The George Washington University, *Leadership Retreat* 67

        University of Memphis, *Board of Visitors* 69

        University of Maryland College Park, Robert H. Smith School of Business, *Dean's Advisory Council and Board of Visitors* 71

        Stetson University, *College of Arts and Sciences Advisory Board* 73

    Advice from the Trenches 75

INDEX 81

ABOUT THE AUTHOR 88

Foreword

IN HIGHER EDUCATION, governing boards differ from advisory councils in some powerful ways, most importantly in the board's sole possession of fiduciary responsibility and legal authority. However, these two bodies also have some significant similarities. Like board members, members of these councils are typically well connected individuals from the community and the alumni, donors, parents, and state government officials. Council members, like board members, are typically recruited for their ability to advise, to share with the institution their considerable intellectual and political capital. And like governing board members, the added ability to support the institution financially can be a compelling reason for an invitation to join the group. Indeed, conventional wisdom says that a strong member of an advisory council is an excellent future member of the board, as a commitment to the institution, a willingness to support it financially, and the ability to contribute to decisions about the institution's future have already been demonstrated.

Despite the significant difference in authority between governing boards and advisory councils, the many similarities can lead to some confusion about the natures and roles of councils: Who identifies the candidates for membership, and who invites them? Where in the institution's organizational chart do these councils reside? Where and in whose budget are they supported? And, what is their charge, their work?

From AGB's 2006 survey, it is clear that advisory councils, which have as many names as they do purposes—such as advisory board, president's circle, and board of visitors to name just a few—operate at many different levels in the institution. Some meet with the president while others meet with deans and faculty. Some have fairly clear responsibilities to help with fundraising while others are asked primarily to give advice on curriculum, help with specialized accreditation, and connect faculty and students with industry. Still others help with recruitment and retention. Many will have a combination of these responsibilities.

Despite or perhaps because of these differences, advisory councils have a growing importance on college and university campuses. Because of changes in the governance environment, some potential board members choose instead to serve institutions through advisory councils. Shrinking state funding levels for higher education have led to needs for stepped up fundraising. Society's demands for higher education to address diverse and growing educational, economic, workforce, and social needs mean that, as Michael Worth says in this book, "Governing boards can no longer do it alone."

Neither can presidents, vice presidents, and deans. The advocacy, advice, contacts, and support supplied by a well run and engaged advisory council add value to the work of an effective institutional leader. A critical challenge is ensuring that capable individuals who volunteer their time to serve on advisory councils believe their time is well spent and their volunteer service matters. The overall challenge is to make the most of the potential of these groups. With *Sounding Boards: Advisory Councils in Higher Education*, Michael Worth provides advice and examples to help ensure that happy result.

Professor of nonprofit management and former vice president for development and alumni affairs at the George Washington University, Michael Worth provides a thoughtful look at advisory councils as well as on-the-ground understanding of the work that engages community, alumni, and campus members in these councils. The result both sheds light on this work and raises the bar on contributions these groups can make to the institutions they serve. This book also offers invaluable guidance to deans, vice presidents, and presidents who are interested in managing their advisory councils and engaging their members more effectively. Comprehensive survey data, case studies, and sample organizing documents supplement solid advice on good practice to make *Sounding Boards* a definitive resource for those who want to establish an advisory council as well as those who want to improve the effectiveness of an existing council.

AGB commends Michael Worth for his interest in the important topic of advisory councils and is grateful to the many presidents and deans who completed the online survey and shared their experiences and opinions. While this volume is limited to information on advisory councils for presidents, deans, and heads or deans of professional schools within a university, we believe the author has broken new ground in this illustrative guide to the myriad volunteer groups that are contributing to the mission of America's universities and colleges. From here, the path lies open to further exploration and study of these important organizational structures in the higher education landscape.

Susan Whealler Johnston
Executive Vice President
Association of Governing Boards
of Universities and Colleges

Preface

SOUNDING BOARDS: ADVISORY COUNCILS IN HIGHER EDUCATION summarizes findings from a 2006 survey conducted by the Association of Governing Boards of Universities and Colleges (henceforth referred to as "the AGB survey" or "the survey") on the purposes, activities, and operations of nearly 500 advisory boards and councils at American public and independent colleges and universities. The survey asked presidents and deans about advisory groups serving entire campuses and those associated with individual colleges and professional schools within universities. Although much of the material came from the survey, I also have included information from interviews with some presidents and deans, materials provided by institutions or drawn from their Web sites, and from my professional experience working with advisory boards and councils as a university administrator. Where relevant, I have noted what is my opinion versus what is the consensus of the presidents and deans surveyed.

AGB surveyed only presidents and deans on their management practices with advisory groups; members of the groups themselves were not included in the study. Consequently, this book is geared toward presidents and deans. It also will appeal to advancement officers and other staff who work with their presidents and deans to manage these groups. The material as well may attract some advisory group members, especially the data concerning how the groups are organized and the types of activities in which they are engaged.

There is evidence that the number of advisory boards and councils is growing. Interest in them also has grown, as AGB reports an increasing number of inquiries from presidents, chancellors, deans, and board members on how to establish and manage such groups. Demand for discussions on the subject at AGB conferences and workshops has grown as well. Until the AGB study, literature on advisory groups has been relatively thin: an AGB-published brochure written by former President Tom Ingram in 1989 and some BoardSource materials that address advisory groups in nonprofit organizations outside of higher education. Nothing previously has provided a comprehensive look at how such groups actually are organized and operated on campuses or has tapped the experience and insight of presidents, chancellors, and deans who are working effectively with such bodies.

By definition, the boards and councils examined in this study do not have the legal responsibility for governing their institutions. However, their roles, activities, and responsibilities—and even the terms by which they are identified—vary widely from one institution to another. Some are purely advisory, while others are engaged in activities that most would associate with "governing." Many are engaged in fundraising, but they are valued also for the advice they provide. Some have links to their institution's governing board, the board of an affiliated foundation, or an alumni association, but the nature of those connections varies and is sometimes complex.

To understand the role of advisory groups and the growing interest in them, it is essential to place them in the broader context of higher education governance and the various pressures affecting college and university governing boards. Chapter 1 discusses trends in higher education governance today and summarizes the types of boards and councils that exist at American colleges and universities. Chapter 2 provides an overview of purposes and roles played by advisory boards and councils. Chapter 3 explores the organization of these groups and describes their size, composition, and other characteristics. Chapter 4 examines how presidents and deans work with their advisory groups and manage their activities, including the pros and cons of different approaches. Chapter 5 offers recommendations to presidents, chancellors, deans, and members of advisory boards and councils, drawn in part from the wisdom of those who participated in the AGB survey. The book concludes with three appendices: examples of advisory group bylaws, case studies of institutions that have successfully worked with advisory groups, and advice from survey participants on how to maximize the value of an advisory group.

X

AGB conducted the survey online and kept responses confidential. Some presidents and deans offered comments on the survey and are quoted anonymously in this book. I also conducted interviews with some presidents and deans and viewed numerous institutional Web sites. Where individuals are quoted by name, it is with their permission. Where individual institutions are mentioned or sample materials included, the information was either provided by the institution with permission for use or was publicly available on its Web site.

I express great thanks to AGB President Richard Legon for his support of this book and the study on which it is based and to Susan Whealler Johnston, executive vice president, who recognized the need for a study of this topic. Merrill Schwartz, director of special projects at AGB, provided invaluable assistance in conducting the survey, and Deanna High, director of AGB Press, ensured the final product would meet AGB's usual high standards. I am grateful as well to the presidents, chancellors, and deans who responded to the AGB survey and to those who shared with me their own experiences. I hope the book will prove useful to them and serve to advance the strength of their important institutions.

Michael J. Worth
Professor of Nonprofit Management
The George Washington University
Washington, D.C.
FEBRUARY 2008

CHAPTER 1

Boards in Higher Education

THE AMERICAN SYSTEM OF HIGHER EDUCATION is generally acknowledged as the finest in the world. It encompasses distinguished research institutions, which provide professional talent and new ideas that drive economic growth and social progress. It includes independent and public four-year campuses, offering diverse philosophies, approaches, and environments to meet the needs of students of varied backgrounds and values. Meanwhile, our extensive system of community colleges addresses the practical needs of employers and students while offering opportunities for advanced study to those who need a transition between high school and college. Although it has its critics, American higher education reflects a rich and diverse array of institutions that have served the needs of the nation and its people well.

The tradition of lay governance is characteristic of American higher education and has been one of its greatest strengths. Colleges and universities in the United States are not governed by faculties or by ministries of education—the predominant models in many parts of the world—but rather by boards of citizens drawn from various walks of life and professions outside the academy. Although some may question whether a corporate model is appropriate for governing "communities of scholars," lay governance has provided important advantages to society and to higher education. For one, governing boards have, for the most part, successfully protected their institutions from political and ideological pressures. Private institutions have diverse sources of revenue, including philanthropy provided by or raised by the board, which help to maintain their independence. At public colleges and universities, appointed or elected boards have provided a buffer between the academy and the state, thus preserving institutional autonomy and academic freedom more effectively than if they were under direct, government control.

Second, lay board members have used their business access, experience, and judgment to ensure their institutions' financial soundness. With independent institutions, board members are often among the largest donors themselves, and they influence others to provide support. They are often the "connectors," who help open doors for the institution with corporate and other sources of funds. For public colleges and universities, board members may be important advocates for state funding. Board members also provide expertise on business matters—for example, real estate and investing that could otherwise be obtained only at a high price.

Finally, lay boards have kept American colleges and universities in tune with the needs and expectations of the business community and the public, preventing them from becoming isolated enclaves and unresponsive to society's needs. Some might prefer colleges and universities to be less market-oriented, less commercialized, and less affected by employer demands, student career aspirations, and donor priorities. Yet, American higher education has always been responsive to vocational and economic concerns. Early private colleges often were affiliated with religious congregations and emphasized preparation for the ministry. States established public colleges and universities in the nineteenth century to meet agricultural research needs and provide technical knowledge for a growing industrial economy. Today, they recognize that investment in their universities is a smart strategy to attract industry and stimulate economic development. Concerns about national and economic security have motivated the federal government's investment in higher education, while disadvantaged groups have sought access to higher education as a means to enter the economic mainstream.

In sum, American colleges and universities have never been isolated scholarly enclaves. They have always responded to the practical needs of government, business, and citizens and served as instruments to achieve society's broader goals, and governance by lay boards has helped ensure they continue to do so. While a different approach to governance might provide institutions and faculty with more freedom to pursue their own directions, it likely would not engender the substantial investment that has sustained the diversity and strength of American higher education as it is today.

The Governing Board's Complex Roles

A S THE OPENING SUGGESTS, governing boards of colleges and universities face complex responsibilities, requiring an array of qualities. The traditional maxim is that board members should provide their institutions with the three Ws: work, wealth, and wisdom. "Work" means simply that board members should invest the time and effort necessary to meet their responsibilities, that they not be absent or passive overseers who lend their names but not their attention. It is a standard similar to the legal requirement that boards exercise "care," that is, that they approach their work with a level of diligence appropriate to their fiduciary responsibilities. "Wisdom" involves making the right judgments and decisions in stewarding the college or university. As boards oversee business and financial matters, they must bring insight and understanding to shape the institution's strategies, directions, and programs so they are consistent with its mission and obligations to its various constituencies. A board's collective wisdom is the sum of the individual capabilities of its members and requires that boards include individuals of diverse talents, experiences, and backgrounds. The board's "wealth"—including the possession of it and/or access to it—is important for its responsibility to ensure the institution's financial strength and future growth.

Finding individuals who are willing to work and who possess wisdom and wealth is an increasing challenge. Once assembled, such boards face myriad, sometimes competing, demands that make their work complex. Governing boards are expected to behave like Janus, the Roman god of doorways and arches, who was said to have the ability to look outward and inward simultaneously. On the one hand, boards have the responsibility to protect and nurture the institutions they serve and to help promote their quality and growth. When performing in that role, board members are the institution's ambassadors to the outside world, serving as its advocates, fundraisers, and protectors against external pressures. At the same time, governing boards also have legal and moral responsibilities to society. They are watchdogs over their institutions, charged with ensuring that colleges and universities efficiently and effectively use their resources and align their programs with society's needs. Chait, Holland, and Taylor have captured the dilemma concisely: "Boards constantly wrestle with when to be 'product champions' and when to be studied neutrals—whether to stand and cheer like rabid partisans when the President of the United States delivers the State of the Union address or to remain seated

2

and stone faced like the Supreme Court justices."[1] In today's higher education environment, growing pressures on boards to be both better champions and better watchdogs—to provide more wisdom and more wealth—have only increased the job's complexity.

Pressures to Compete

COLLEGES AND UNIVERSITIES ARE COMPETITIVE ENTERPRISES, and competition has become intense. Government funding for higher education has shifted in recent decades from institutional support to student aid. Prospective students have become consumers, requiring institutions to compete for their business. Although competition for top students is keen at both independent and public institutions, tuition-dependent independent institutions especially are concerned with achieving the desired size and quality of student body. At the same time, they face resistance to tuition increases, as students and their families have become informed consumers and demand the best educational value. Philanthropy is increasingly important to provide resources for both current operating needs and long-term investments for facilities, equipment, and endowment.

Public colleges and universities have faced increased competition for appropriated funds, as state legislatures juggle growing demands to fund transportation infrastructure, law enforcement, and social programs devolved from the federal level. Consequently, public institutions have had to increase tuition while intensifying efforts to secure philanthropic support. Indeed, in the past three decades, public colleges and universities have virtually closed the fundraising gap with their private counterparts. As the Voluntary Support of Education survey reveals, almost half of the top 20 institutions that received private voluntary support in 2005 were public universities.[2]

Meanwhile, many foundations have shifted their interests from higher education to international efforts addressing the environment, health, and children. Many corporations have transitioned from philanthropy to partnerships based on the mutual interests of the company and the organizations it supports. At the same time, individual and family wealth has increased exponentially, and a new generation of individual philanthropists has made national headlines with blockbuster gifts to colleges, universities, and other entities. In this environment, individual donor gifts—especially major gifts—have become critical to both independent and public colleges and universities. Institutions are seeking to connect with these potentially major donors and are turning to board members, both for their own support and for help in engaging others of substantial means.

The leadership of boards in giving and raising funds is essential, and it is the reality that many individual philanthropists give to organizations on whose boards they serve. According to the Council for Aid to Education (CASE), board gifts account for more than 20 percent of all individual giving to private higher education institutions.[3] Furthermore, a 2004 AGB study found that trustees are involved in identifying, cultivating, and soliciting donors at the overwhelming majority of colleges and universities. The increased competition for resources, and especially for individual philanthropy, has led some boards to establish give-or-get policies for board members and to place increased emphasis on enlisting new trustees who possess both affluence and influence.

1   Richard P. Chait, Thomas P. Holland, and Barbara E. Taylor, *Improving the Performance of Governing Boards* (Phoenix, Ariz.: Oryx Press, 1996), 3.

2   Council for Aid to Education, *Voluntary Support of Education*, 2005 (New York: Council for Aid to Education, 2005).

3   Ibid.

3

Demands for Accountability

AT THE SAME TIME, society is demanding that boards improve their oversight of the institutions they govern. The public expects colleges and universities to operate with integrity, efficiency, and effectiveness while providing programs that meet society's needs.

Corporate scandals, such as Enron's, have heightened awareness and stimulated discussion of board oversight responsibilities in all sectors, including higher education. Although Congress passed the Sarbanes-Oxley Act of 2002 to hold publicly traded companies to higher standards of accountability, some states have enacted similar legislation aimed at nonprofit organizations. Meanwhile, highly publicized governance issues at national nonprofit organizations, including the American Red Cross and the Nature Conservancy, captured the attention of Senator Charles Grassley (R-Iowa), then-chairman of the Senate Finance Committee. He proposed new federal legislation to strengthen nonprofit accountability. The discussion extended to higher education in the fall of 2005, when the president of American University in Washington, D.C. was accused of using university funds to support a lavish lifestyle. Some blamed the university's board for a lack of appropriate oversight; the trustees split into factions, and their debate spilled onto the front pages of the Washington Post. Senator Grassley launched an investigation and again pushed for new legislation to demand greater accountability from governing boards. Recognizing the threat of federal action, AGB issued a report in early 2007 calling for more self-regulation by higher education boards "before rigid external regulation pre-empts responsive internal action.[4]

A Rock and a Hard Place

IN THE ENVIRONMENT DESCRIBED ABOVE, colleges and universities, and their boards, find themselves in the proverbial spot between a rock and a hard place. Trustees are asked to give and raise more money—to be stronger and more energetic champions of their institutions—while also becoming more aggressive in their oversight of its finances and management. Wealth and access to wealth are important criteria for selecting new board members, but the pressure to govern better requires boards to include individuals with various specialized skills to monitor the institution's programs and finances while also reflecting the diversity of the institution and its constituents.

Understanding the connection between board service and giving, presidents and chief advancement or development officers seek to engage the active participation of larger numbers of affluent alumni and business leaders to cultivate their interest and support. However, not all can serve on the governing board; indeed, many experts argue that smaller boards do a more effective job of governing. In public institutions, the size and composition of the governing board may be determined by law, limiting presidents' ability to influence the profile of individuals appointed or elected to serve. University deans, who a generation ago were academic leaders without significant responsibilities for fundraising, now devote almost as much time to cultivating and soliciting gifts as do their presidents and chancellors. They also understand the importance of board leadership in fundraising and must work with such a group to achieve the goals of their colleges and professional schools.

In sum, faced with such competing and increasing pressures, governing boards can

---

4   "AGB Statement on Accountability," adopted by the AGB Board of Directors January 17, 2007, (Washington, D.C.: AGB, 2007).

no longer do it alone. As former AGB President Tom Ingram writes, "Contemporary education organizations require the eyes and ears, commitment and dedication, skill and expertise of many more lay volunteers than we find on the legally constituted governing board."[5] Indeed, most campuses now have affiliated with them a variety of other external groups that provide varying degrees of wealth and wisdom to supplement and support the governing board. They vary widely in their roles, responsibilities, and activities, and they sometimes have complicated relationships with the other boards. Some have explicit legal responsibilities; others have responsibilities delegated to them by the governing board, while others serve exclusively as advisors and advocates with varying degrees of formality in their structure and operation. As Ingram suggests, what exists at many campuses today is a "governance continuum, ranging from the governing board to various quasi-governing groups to…advisory groups."

5

---

5   Richard T. Ingram, "Making Advisory Committees and Boards Work," Pocket Publication Series, (Washington, D.C.: AGB, 1989), 2.

TYPES OF BOARDS

TABLE 1.0 Types of Boards and Councils

Governing boards
• Independent colleges and universities
• Single-campus public colleges and universities
• Statewide systems of colleges and universities
Institutionally related foundation boards
• State university systems
• Single campus of a multicampus university
• College or school within a university
• Specific programs, such as athletics
Alumni association boards
• Independent alumni associations
• Dependent alumni associations (unincorporated)
• Interdependent alumni associations
Advisory boards and councils
• Institution or campus (for example, President's Council, President's Advisory Board)
• College or school within a university (for example, Dean's Council, Dean's Board of Advisors)
• Department, program, discipline
Donor recognition societies
• Automatic "membership" to recognize donor giving at specific levels (for example, "President's Council," "Dean's Circle," and so forth)
• Informal, not truly "organizations"

GOVERNING BOARDS. The legally constituted governing board defines one end of the governance continuum, holding full authority and responsibility for the institution. At independent colleges and universities, the governing board is most commonly called the board of trustees. Most are self-perpetuating, meaning that the board itself selects new members; some have ex-officio members, often including the president. Some independent institutions use more complex models. For example, Harvard University has two boards. The President and Fellows of Harvard College, also known as the Harvard Corporation, is the university's executive board with responsibility for finances and important educational policy decisions. A Board of Overseers, elected by alumni of Harvard and Radcliffe, provides advice to the President and Fellows and is required to approve certain of their actions, including major academic and administrative appointments.

At public institutions, governing boards are generally appointed by the governor with confirmation by the state legislature, although in some states, the public elects members of the state university board. Many also have ex-officio members, including the president and perhaps public officials, who serve by virtue of their position.

Some public campuses have independent governing boards, while others are part of statewide systems (or are part of a multicampus university), in which a single board governs all the campuses. For example, the Board of Regents of the University of California comprises eighteen governor-appointed individuals, one student member, and seven ex-officio members including state officials and two officers of the alumni association. Established in the state constitution, the Board of Regents has full authority for the university system's ten campuses, except for some specific areas of control retained by the legislature. In some state systems, individual institutions have local advisory boards in addition to the system board, and those that play a role in governance are sometimes called "quasi-governing boards." They will be discussed further below.

HISTORICALLY, governing boards of public colleges and universities have not been important sources of philanthropic support or fundraising leadership for their institutions. Many are smaller than independent institution boards, and the political nature of their appointment does not ensure that members are either personally affluent or closely connected with sources of wealth. Some boards include public officials who may be ethically or legally constrained in their ability to raise funds. In addition, many states require public board meetings, a practice that inhibits the discussion of fundraising and makes it difficult to accept gifts from donors who wish anonymity or to have the terms of their gifts kept private. For those reasons and others, as private support has become more critical to public institutions, institutionally related foundations have increased in number and importance.

In *Margin of Excellence: The New Work of Higher Education Foundations*, AGB President Richard Legon identifies more than 1,500 foundations at public college and university campuses. Most serve a single campus, although some serve an entire statewide system. Some universities—for example, the University of Virginia and University of North Carolina—host multiple foundations focused on raising and managing private funds for individual colleges, schools, and other units. Athletic foundations are also common and have a long history at state universities. Finally, some universities have separate research foundations that manage grants and contracts.

An institutionally related foundation is a 501(c)(3) organization separate from the public college or university it supports. The foundation has its own governing board, which has legal responsibility for the funds managed by the foundation and, in some cases, for the hiring of the foundation's staff.

Some institutionally related foundations are independent. They employ their own staffs and meet all of their own costs. Others are considered interdependent; they provide some of their own operating resources and receive support from the host institution. Some are dependent, meaning the host institution closely controls them, as they function as the fundraising arm of the college or university. The question of independence has been the focus of recent legal cases about disclosure of information by the foundation, with the most sensitive issues related to private donor records. In general, the more independent the foundation, the stronger its defense against demands for disclosure, but there are also tradeoffs in terms of the institution's loss of control. A full discussion of the issues is beyond the scope of this book, but they have heightened the visibility of foundation board responsibilities.

Foundation boards are more than advisory with regard to the foundation; they have legal responsibility for the funds it raises and manages. As host institutions increasingly rely on these resources, foundations have become more influential on campus. The foundation board, however, is not the governing board of the institution itself. Maintaining good relationships between the two may require some effort, and there have been cases of friction that have proven embarrassing and destructive to both the foundation and the institution it serves.

As Legon writes, "Foundation boards must recognize that their host institution's governing board bears ultimate authority for establishing institutional priorities and policies. Broadened foundation board responsibility should not be confused with a greater role in institutional governance. Presidents walk a tightrope as they draw on the talents and influence of foundation board members while ensuring that the foundation board does not usurp the authority of the governing board." [6]

ALUMNI ASSOCIATION BOARDS. Alumni associations have a long and distinguished history in American higher education, dating back to 1792, when Yale began to collect and publish "notes" on the activities of its graduates. Williams College and Princeton University organized alumni in the 1820s with state universities soon after. The University of Michigan's alumni association, created in 1897, became the first to hire a full-time alumni secretary whose salary was paid by alumni rather than the university.

Like institutionally related foundations, alumni associations vary in degrees of autonomy from their institutions. Some are independently incorporated and thus are legally separate from the college or university. Some of them are also financially independent, supporting their staffing and program needs entirely through dues revenue and earned income. The number of independent alumni associations has decreased in recent years. Other alumni associations are interdependent. They may be incorporated and have some independent sources of revenue, but they also receive support from their institutions, usually including the services of alumni relations employees of the college or university. Dependent alumni associations are not incorporated and are often informal organizations closely related to the alumni relations office of the institution. In many universities, there are institutionwide alumni associations as well as constituent associations for specific colleges or professional schools within the university. Many colleges and universities also have local alumni association chapters or clubs offering events and services to alumni in a particular city or region. Most of those are not incorporated and have boards and officers that do not have legal authority or responsibilities.

Like the boards of institutionally related foundations, boards of incorporated alumni associations have legal responsibilities for the association's finances, but they are not the governing boards of their institutions. Some alumni associations, however, do nominate governing board members and, depending on the provisions of institutional bylaws or tradition, elect them. Unlike institutionally related foundations, which exist only to raise and manage private funds, many alumni associations do not engage in substantial fundraising. Rather, they operate programs to benefit alumni or more broadly engage, involve, and inform alumni with the goal of engendering their assistance to the campus. This assistance includes not only giving, but also advocacy to state governments (for public universities) and student recruitment (for independent institutions). Some institutions also have "alumni advisory boards" or something similarly named. Many of these are not alumni association boards; rather, they are advisory councils (like those discussed below), which limit their membership to alumni of the institution.

ADVISORY BOARDS AND COUNCILS. The groups this book focuses on are advisory boards and councils that are associated with an entire institution or with a specific college or professional school within a university. Although there are wide variations in practice, these boards or councils have the following characteristics:

---

6 Richard D. Legon, *Margin of Excellence: The New Work of Higher Education Foundations* (Washington, D.C., Association of Governing Boards of Universities and Colleges, 2005.

- *They are external.* Some may include faculty or other internal members, but their membership primarily comprises individuals from outside the campus.

- *Membership is selective.* Members are elected or appointed through some process. Membership is not automatic as a result of making a gift, although it is common for major donors to be selected for service.

- *They do not have governing authority.* They may exist to provide advice, advocacy, fundraising assistance, and other services to the institution. Some have formal bylaws and operate in a highly structured way. Some may have influence and be quasi-governing. They are not the governing boards of their institutions, however, nor do they have legal responsibility for a foundation or an incorporated alumni association.

- *They serve an entire institution or a college or professional school within a university.* College and university campuses host multiple advisory groups; the only ones included in the AGB survey were those that provide high-level advice directly to the president or to a dean. Those related to academic departments or disciplines, sometimes called "program committees," were not included. Nevertheless, the findings and management practices recommended in this book may prove useful to them. Another advisory group excluded from the survey was the internal advisory board or council that represents staff, students, or faculty and that provides advice to the president or dean. While the dynamics of such groups may be similar to those of the councils discussed in this book, they are inherently different, because they encompass individuals who are employees of the institution and generally do not have external roles. Finally, donor recognition clubs or societies— often called the "president's (or dean's) council" or something similar, even using the term "advisory"—are not included in this book, as membership is given automatically to donors at a specified giving level.

More than one-third of the presidents responding to the AGB survey have an advisory group at the institutionwide level, with about the same percentage in independent and public institutions. The vast majority of deans surveyed—73 percent at independent universities and 78 percent at public universities—reported having an advisory group associated with their college or school, not including those groups that may pertain to specific academic departments, programs, centers, and other units. In total, participants described 482 different advisory groups, likely a fraction of all that exist throughout higher education.

It seems logical that presidents find less need for advisory groups than deans do, as presidents have direct access to their governing boards and, at many public institutions, the board of an institutionally related foundation. At some public institutions, the foundation board likely plays a role similar to that of an advisory board or council. (The survey specifically directed presidents to exclude foundation boards from their responses.) Deans are likely to have less contact with the institution's governing or foundation boards and thus may find it more useful to have an advisory council associated directly with their schools.

The advisory groups go by a variety of names. The most common (42 percent of all the groups reported) includes the word "council," for example, the president's council or the dean's council. Another 38 percent are called "boards," such as dean's board of advisors, president's advisory board, and the like. Six percent are called the board of visitors, which is also the name of the governing board at some institutions. The remainder are known by various

9

titles, including president's roundtable, board of associates, president's or dean's circle, advocates, and counselors.

The variations in terminology can be confusing. For example, while the board of visitors is the legal governing board of the University of Virginia, the board of visitors at independent Davidson College is an advisory group; Davidson's governing board is its board of trustees. A board of regents governs the University of California system, but the board of regents at independent Georgetown University is not the principal governing board. That responsibility is held by a smaller group, called the president and directors of Georgetown College. While the board of overseers at Harvard has a role in governing, the overseers at the Tuck School of Dartmouth University "are responsible for advising the dean on the strategic direction and mission of the institution."

Nancy Axelrod, who has written for BoardSource on the role of advisory groups in nonprofit organizations, suggests that it would be best to distinguish "boards" from "councils," using the former only for groups that have legal governing authority and reserving the latter for purely advisory groups. While there is much to recommend Axelrod's suggestion, the reality is that both terms are used widely in higher education. Interestingly, more than 67 percent of the independent institution presidents who responded to the survey and have an advisory group said their groups are known as "councils," perhaps to distinguish them from the governing boards with which they directly work. However, deans—both in public and independent institutions—were somewhat more likely to identify their advisory groups as "boards," perhaps because their affiliation with a specific college or school is sufficient to distinguish them from the institution's governing board. To keep things simple, this book refers to these groups as either, "advisory boards and councils" or "councils," as most easily fits the context.

As discussed previously, advisory boards and councils are positioned across a governance continuum. Some are purely advisory; others have more formalized roles. Some have specific responsibilities delegated by the governing board and are considered quasi-governing. Boards with quasi-governing powers are sometimes found at campus-affiliated adjunct enterprises, such as radio and television stations, museums, and medical research centers. In addition, a number of public institutions that are part of systems (and campuses within multicampus institutions) have local boards that may participate in governance-type activities, including evaluation of the president and presidential searches. Some local boards of public campuses exist in statute, or in the bylaws of the system's governing board, and some have members who are politically appointed. Others are more informal and are appointed by the president or chancellor of the campus; even then, some may have influence on certain decisions and may participate in activities that are quasi-governing in nature.

Advisory boards and councils may have some influence in searches and other decisions even at independent institutions. Points along the governance continuum are often quite close together, and the distinctions among advising, influencing, and quasi-governing can be minimal.

The Question of Liability

SOME SEE THE POTENTIAL FOR LEGAL LIABILITY associated with governing board service as one reason for the increasing numbers of advisory councils. Although there has been no research, some speculate that individuals may prefer to serve on advisory councils, where they can help with fundraising and benefit the institution with their expertise without the legal risks that come with fiduciary responsibility.

However, Ingram and Axelrod, who have both written about advisory councils, agree that advisory council members do face some risk. The more quasi-governing the advisory council is—and especially if it plays a role in personnel decisions—the greater the personal exposure its members may have. Ingram advises council members to adhere to the same duties of care, diligence, loyalty, prudence, and ethics as would apply if they were on the governing board. Also, institutions should cover their council members under the same liability insurance they provide for their governing board members.

Relationships Among Boards

AS DISCUSSED ABOVE, relationships among an institution's various boards and councils can be complex and sometimes sensitive. This has been particularly visible in some celebrated cases of institutionally related foundation boards that have come into conflict with the governing boards of their host institutions. Boundaries among the various board and council roles may not always be clear. For example, some presidents at public campuses undoubtedly turn to their foundation or alumni association boards as a source of advice, so they are "advisory boards" as well as the governing boards of the foundation or alumni association.

Membership among various boards and councils may overlap; that is, some individuals may serve the institution in multiple capacities. Having overlapping membership among the various groups may help improve communication and avoid tension. However, if individuals fail to distinguish their roles when serving in various capacities, the overlap can be confusing. This point will be discussed further below.

On some campuses, alumni association boards, advisory councils, and governing boards are linked by having members of one serve ex-officio on others. For example, the chair of Georgetown's Board of Regents serves as an ex-officio member of its Board of Directors. Wartburg College, in Waverly, Iowa, has national advisory boards associated with its academic programs and departments, including the Iowa Broadcasting Archives, the business department, the communication arts department, diversity programs, the leadership program, the library, Pathways Center, the social work department, and the vocations program. The advisory boards are linked to the governing Board of Regents through a President's Advisory Council. Wartburg's Web site explains:

> The advisory boards have a direct reporting link to the Board of Regents
> through the President's Advisory Council (PAC), which serves as an over-
> sight group to review recommendations of the advisory boards and act as
> a sounding board on issues that are central to the entire campus. The chair
> of the PAC serves as a member of the Board of Regents. Membership on the
> PAC [comprises] chairpersons of each national advisory council and "at large"
> members who represent a wide range of expertise and disciplines.[7]

The AGB survey asked presidents and deans at public institutions about membership overlaps between institutionally related foundation boards and advisory boards or councils. (Most independent institutions do not have such foundations.) Close to all—96 percent—of the presidents reported having a related foundation. Of those who have both a foundation and an advisory council, 73 percent said that the memberships of the two groups are completely

11

---

7   Wartburg College, "President's Advisory Council," *http://www.wartburg.edu/about/advcouncil.html* (accessed February 19, 2007).

separate, while 13 percent said there is some overlap. Of the deans who responded, only 36 percent have a foundation that serves only their individual school or college. While 52 percent said there is no overlap at all, 31 percent reported some overlap, and 6 percent said the overlap is significant.

What about governing board members who also serve on a separate advisory board or council? Both independent and public institution presidents—25 percent and 27 percent, respectively—reported some governing board members serve on their advisory councils. Responses from independent university deans, however, significantly differed from those at public universities. Almost 34 percent of deans at independent universities reported their school advisory councils included at least some members of the institution's governing board, but only 16 percent of the deans at public campuses have governing board members on their advisory councils.

There may be some real advantages to a college or professional school having governing board members serve on its council. It facilitates communication between the governing board and advisory council. It may also help to enhance the prestige of the advisory council, making it easier to recruit strong, new members. Also, it may help develop the advisory council as a "farm club" for the governing board, enabling council members to demonstrate their skill and commitment while providing the governing board with a source of strong candidates to join its ranks.

Despite the advantages mentioned above, overlap among the membership of boards and councils also can be challenging. Conflicts of interest may arise if trustees serving as advisory council members begin to advocate for a particular college or school. They would be neglecting their fiduciary responsibility to the overall institution, which could lead to serious governance issues for the president and the university. If a president or dean wishes to engage more people as the institution's advocates, it does not make sense to repeatedly ask the same people to serve on multiple boards and councils.

Key Findings from the 2006 AGB Survey

THE FOLLOWING LIST PROVIDES AN OVERVIEW of key findings from the AGB survey. In later chapters, we will explore issues in greater depth.

- More than one-third of the presidents responding to the survey have an advisory group at the institutionwide level, with about the same percentage in independent and public institutions. The vast majority of deans surveyed—73 percent at independent universities and 78 percent at public universities—reported having an advisory group associated with their college or school, not including additional groups that may be related to specific academic departments, programs, centers, and other units.

- Seventy-eight percent of presidents and 81 percent of deans said their advisory councils are helpful to the university, college, or school.

- Forty-two percent of the groups include the word "council" in their names—for example, the President's Council or the Dean's Council. Another 38 percent are called "boards," such as Dean's Board of Advisors and President's Advisory Board. Another 6 percent are called the Board of Visitors, and the remainder go by various other designations.

- Most advisory councils have 11 to 30 members.

- The most common constituencies represented on the vast majority of advisory councils are alumni, donors and prospects other than alumni, corporate executives, and local community leaders.

- Almost two-thirds of advisory councils have formal bylaws and/or formal job descriptions that specify their responsibilities, membership, and terms of service.

- The typical job description for advisory council members includes the following responsibilities: serving as advocates and ambassadors for the institution; increasing the institution's visibility and reputation; providing advice to the president or dean; providing nonfinancial assistance, such as career counseling for students; and making and helping to secure gifts.

- Presidents most value their councils as a way to try out new people as future members of the governing board, for their fundraising help, and as a way to improve external relationships with people other than donors. Deans rank advice, external relationships, and fundraising as the three most valuable purposes of their councils.

- Fundraising is an important purpose of many councils, but most do not require a minimum annual gift of members.

- In more than 60 percent of cases, the president or dean appoints members of advisory councils. In some cases, the president appoints college or school advisory councils upon the dean's recommendation.

- Sixty-four percent of institutionwide advisory councils and 73 percent of college or school advisory boards have a chair. In about half the cases, the president or dean selects the chair and about one-third are elected by council members.

- Most advisory councils do not have fixed terms of service or term limits. Those that do typically have two- or three-year terms, renewable two or three times.

- Most institutionwide advisory councils receive staff support from the advancement or development office. A member of the dean's staff supports the college and school councils in most cases, although some are supported by the school's advancement office.

- The president's office budget funds most institutionwide council activities, while the dean's budget funds most college and school councils.

- Most council meetings include presentations on the institution's programs, discussions about the institution's strategic issues, and social activities. Discussion of fundraising goals and prospects is sometimes on the agenda.

- In offering advice on starting or working with an advisory council, presidents and deans emphasize defining clearly the council's purpose; maintaining clear understanding of the distinction between advising and governing; selecting the right people to serve; and engaging in discussion and dialogue rather than just making presentations to the council.

Questions for Presidents, Chancellors, and Deans

- Are your council members well informed about the overall structure of governance at your institution and the respective roles of various boards and councils?

- Have you made an effort to ensure that the members of all your institution's boards and councils clearly understand their responsibilities and authority in relation to other groups?

- If some individuals serve on more than one board or council at your institution, do they keep those roles properly separate and remain mindful of the roles of other groups?

CHAPTER 2

Purposes and Roles of Advisory Boards and Councils

WHY ESTABLISH OR MAINTAIN AN ADVISORY BOARD or council? What purposes and roles do they serve? What benefits do they bring to their institutions, and why would individuals wish to serve on groups that do not have governing authority? Let's consider the individuals first, then look at the purposes of advisory councils and the value they bring to their institutions.

Why People Serve

THE AGB SURVEY DID NOT EXPLORE the motivations of individual board and council members, but several authors have discussed why people serve on boards. The reasons are similar to why donors give: they are varied and often mixed, ranging from altruistic and noble motivations to the practical.

First, as all but the most cynical will recognize, people serve on boards and make philanthropic gifts because they feel an obligation to contribute to institutions that have influenced their loved ones or themselves and that they believe are important to the future of society. Most board members are good people who give their time and expertise to try and make a positive difference.

Individuals also may serve on baords for practical reasons. For example, some participate at the encouragement of their employers, who find an association with a university useful for learning about new research or for recruiting top graduates. Others may be interested in networking, possibly leading to business opportunities through other board members. Serving on a board may, in fact, be an expectation of those who occupy prominent positions in business or the community. In Francie Ostrower's study of wealthy donors, one participant shared, "I am a trustee of a hospital. You have to be a trustee of a hospital if you're wealthy. It's required."[1] The same could be said of serving on the boards of colleges and universities, among the most respected institutions in our society, but it also carries considerable prestige and may enhance one's social position in the community. Board membership conveys the impression of "having arrived," socially as well as financially, and suggests that individuals are sought for their intellect and judgment. As fundraising consultant Harold "Si" Seymour wrote more than forty years ago, to be sought as a worthwhile member of a worthwhile (or prestigious) group is a fundamental human social need.[2]

Individuals also may serve on a board or council because it can be an inherently interesting and broadening experience. When I was a university vice president, I once asked

---

1   Francie Ostrower, *Why the Wealthy Give: The Culture of Elite Philanthropy* (Princeton, N.J.: Princeton University Press, 1995), 36.

2   Harold J. Seymour, *Designs for Fundraising: Principles, Patterns, Techniques* (New York: McGraw Hill, 1966).

a new trustee, who was a business person, what he thought of his first university board meeting. "Well," the man replied, "it was interesting, but I'm a little disappointed." When asked why, he explained, "It was a very well-run meeting, and I am impressed by what the university administration is doing, but it was a lot like the corporate board meetings that I attend all the time—a lot of discussion about budgets and projections and so forth. I live with that kind of discussion everyday, and I was hoping the university board might provide something different, something more stimulating." His comments provide new insight. Some people join college or university boards—whether governing boards or advisory councils—because they are looking for something different in their lives: perhaps a set of problems, different from their professional pursuits, to which they can apply their expertise and talent; perhaps intellectual stimulation from discussions with academics; and perhaps camaraderie with other board members. The insight is an important consideration in planning what an advisory board or council should do and how its meetings should unfold. It suggests that show-and-tell PowerPoints may impress, but they may not provide the kind of interaction that members find rewarding.

Some speculate that fewer individuals may be willing to serve on governing boards than in years past, given the demands and risks of trusteeship in today's Sarbanes-Oxley climate. Others argue that many boards should be smaller anyway to govern more effectively. In a provocative article in the *Stanford Social Innovation Review*, Michael Klausner and Jonathon Small argue that many boards do not govern as effectively as today's expectations require, in part because they are too large.[3] They suggest that some members of large boards may be tempted "to free ride on the efforts of others.... Why study the details of a proposed budget if 39 other board members or at least some of them (hopefully) will?"[4] They point out that sometimes, board members are there for purposes of fundraising, giving advice, or even just "lending their names" to help bring visibility to the institution. They cannot be expected to give their full effort and attention to the tasks that governing today requires. To solve this problem, Klausner and Small propose the "bifurcated board," on which some members have a fiduciary responsibility and others do not. They describe, "The objective of the bifurcated board structure is to make the governance role clear to the board members who assume governance responsibility and to the public, while also continuing to use the board for fundraising and other non-governance functions."[5] The purposes Klausner and Small describe for the bifurcated board might, of course, be served also by making governing boards smaller and surrounding them with advisory boards and councils of increased standing and importance.

Again, AGB's survey did not contact council members themselves, so it cannot determine whether individuals indeed have become more concerned with governing responsibilities, as observers suggest. To the extent that such concern exists, expanding the number and role of advisory councils may provide institutions with a strategy for involving more people whose help and advice they need without the obligations of serving on a governing or foundation board. As one president responded to AGB's survey, "The advisory council provides a place for those who can help the college but are unable or unwilling to commit the time that [governing] board membership would require." Membership on an advisory board or council provides many of the same satisfactions as serving on a board that has greater responsibility—the sense of making an important contribution, the chance to develop new relationships, and the inherent enjoyment of participating in the academic community. However, this requires

---

3   Michael Klausner and Jonathan Small, "Failing to Govern?: The Disconnect Between Theory and Reality in Nonprofit Boards and How to Fix It," *Stanford Social Innovation Review* 3 (Spring 2005).

4   Ibid.

5   Ibid.

the advisory council experience to offer something more than opportunities for giving funds and listening to presentations. It must offer a real role in influencing the direction and future of the institution.

Advisory Board and Council Responsibilities

IF THERE ARE MULTIPLE REASONS why individuals might wish to serve on college and university boards, what value do institutions derive from them? The answer may be clear with regard to a governing or foundation board—they have explicit and essential responsibilities and authority. Most advisory councils do not have authority, except when delegated by a governing board. Most job descriptions thus speak not about authority, but the responsibilities of the council and its members.

The mission statements or job descriptions of advisory boards and councils at colleges and universities, many of which are available on the Web, describe a number of common responsibilities, including:

- Becoming well-informed about the institution's programs, thus serving as its *ambassadors* and *advocates*. Most call for council members to be advocates within their respective professional and social circles and, in the case of graduate or professional schools, as advocates for the school within the larger university (for example, the Columbia Law School Board of Visitors).

- Providing *advice* to the president, chancellor, or dean. Some descriptions refer specifically to advice on curriculum and academic matters, but many say the council advises on strategic issues.

- Increasing the institution's *visibility* and *image*. Similar to their roles as ambasadors, board members are "authenticators" for their institutions. In other words, having prominent and respected individuals visibly associated with the college or university adds credibility and luster to its image.

- Bringing specific *nonfinancial resources* to the institution. For example, the Methodist University Board of Visitors is responsible for helping to recruit students and providing guest lecturers. The McCombs School of Business expects Advisory Council members to help faculty expand their contacts in the business community to enhance their teaching and research.

- *Participating* in meetings and school events. For example, the Board of Visitors of the Drucker and Ito School at Claremont Graduate University specifically identifies attendance at meetings and events as among members' responsibilities.

- Providing gifts and helping in *fundraising*. Most council job descriptions obliquely mention fundraising responsibilities, often referring to helping identify donors or assisting the president or dean in cultivating donor prospects. We will have a fuller discussion of the advisory council role in fundraising below.

In sum, based on the typical council mission statement or job description, it appears that colleges and universities, like the individuals who serve them, may have more than one benefit in mind.

17

VALUE OF ADVISORY COUNCILS

TO DETERMINE WHAT BENEFITS institutions actually derive from advisory councils, the AGB survey asked presidents and deans to rate the value of their councils with respect to various purposes and activities, drawn from typical advisory council mission statements. They used a 5-point scale on which "5" means "extremely valuable" and "1" means "of no value at all." Table 2.0 shows the mean scores for each category of respondent.

TABLE 2.0 Responses of Presidents and Deans on the Value of Advisory Boards and Councils

	Mean score			
	Independent institution presidents	Public institution presidents	Independent institution deans	Public institution deans
As a way to involve more people who will give and help with fundraising	**3.48**	2.60	**3.32**	**3.63**
As a way to "try out" people before adding them to the institution's governing board or to the foundation board	**3.58**	1.93	2.56	2.03
As a source of advice to the president or dean	3.13	3.49	3.82	3.88
As a source of advice on curriculum	2.16	1.86	3.01	2.91
As a source of "political" leverage within the institution	1.81	2.40	2.88	3.18
As a way to gain better relationships with outside constituencies other than donors	3.16	**3.67**	**3.37**	**3.80**
As a way to involve people who may not want the legal responsibilities of serving on a governing or foundation board	2.53	**2.67**	NA	2.16
As a way to help recruit students	2.31	1.93	2.45	2.41
As a way to help students find jobs or internships	2.68	2.27	3.29	3.24
As a way to help provide research or consulting opportunities for faculty	1.72	1.79	2.34	2.47

Scale: 1 = of no value, 2 = of some value, 3 = valuable, 4 = very valuable, 5 = extremely valuable
Note: Bold figures indicate top three responses for each category of respondent.

The responses defy any who might think that the only purpose of advisory councils is to involve potential donors and fundraising leaders. Both presidents and deans—in both private and public institutions—identified other purposes as more valuable, although fundraising ranked in the top three for all of them.

Both presidents and deans highly value the help their advisory councils provide in building external relationships with individuals other than donors, including government officials, local community residents, and parents of students. Not surprisingly, public university presidents most value the help their councils provide in building relationships with external constituencies other than donors, including important government officials. On the other hand, independent institution presidents, who generally have more influence over governing board appointments and who are generally less concerned about relationships with government, most value advisory councils as a way to try out new people who eventually may join the governing board. As might be expected, deans ranked highest the assistance their advisory councils provide to students and faculty.

COUNCILS AS "FARM CLUBS." Many presidents and deans have the ability to appoint individuals to serve on an advisory council without obtaining their election, or even their approval, by others. This may be an easy first step to involve someone who has the potential to become a major donor or who might provide an important relationship with a local community or industry. In contrast, asking someone to join the governing board is a complicated process requiring time and thoughtful consideration. It's a little like proposing marriage on a first date, an invitation that most people would not accept and that most prudent individuals would not extend without some additional shared experience. Inviting individuals to join an advisory council, however, can be a low-risk way of determining whether they will indeed take an interest in the institution and participate in its work and whether they will be a good fit with the culture of the institution and its trustees. As one president explained, "If advisory council members show a willingness to donate time and money, then they may be good candidates for the governing board."

19

The advisory council also may provide opportunities for members of a governing or foundation board to become better acquainted with individuals and assess their candidacy to assume greater responsibility. This is facilitated if trustees serve on advisory councils or if the councils and the governing board have some shared activities and events. Of course, advisory board service also allows individuals to decide if the institution is right for them without assuming the significant workload and responsibility of trusteeship. Having an advisory council as a trial for governing board service thus can help make the process more deliberate and thoughtful, for both parties involved.

Of course, presidents of public institutions generally have less influence on appointments to their governing boards than do presidents of independent colleges and universities. However, they may have a role in selecting members of a foundation board, and advisory councils may help in that process.

According to deans' survey responses, they are less likely than presidents to value their advisory council as a farm club for the governing board, which is understandable because most deans have less interaction with the governing board than do presidents. Still, some deans mentioned the value of having trustees on the council and the benefits to the school when council members advance to the governing board. Advisory councils also could provide a stepping stone to a college or school foundation board.

COUNCILS AS ADVISORS. Both independent and public institution deans gave their top rating to their councils as a source of advice. Presidents also ranked advice relatively high, although less so than deans, perhaps because they have more sources of external input, including their governing boards.

Reflecting on the value of the advisory council's advice, one president noted that the president works for the governing board and thus may not feel free to use it as a sounding board for new ideas or for "thinking out loud" about problems facing the institution. However, "the advisory council provides opportunities for the president to have confidential conversations with seasoned leaders who are not involved in evaluating his or her performance." A dean at a public university also pointed to the value of the council as a confidential sounding board "when I have ideas and do not want to share them with the greater university community."

The advice that presidents and deans value the most, according to the survey, is that which involves "broad policies and programs" rather than curriculum. While deans were more likely than presidents to value their council for its advice on curriculum matters, some also clarified that department or program-focused advisory councils play a larger role in that area than does the schoolwide dean's council.

In comments responding to the AGB survey, more than one dean or president advised against engaging councils in curriculum matters. One respondent noted that faculty controls curriculum; consequently, it might be difficult to implement the council's advice. However, professional schools, such as business and engineering, sometimes welcome the council's input on curriculum with the view that it helps prepare students for the real needs of industry. For example, the Board of Visitors at the Duke University Fuqua School of Business has an explicit charge to provide advice on curriculum, not only to the school but also to the university's governing board:

> The function of Fuqua's board of visitors is to provide information and recommendations to the committee for academic affairs of Duke University's board of trustees on matters relating to the Fuqua School of Business. This board gives informal advice and assistance to the school about the curriculum, facilities, operations, and any other matter deemed appropriate by the board of visitors. Their primary goal is to promote better communication with the business community, as well as with other constituencies.[6]

Some presidents and deans described their advisory council's role in planning. One dean wrote, "Our advisory board has three committees, each tied to a component of the college's strategic plan. They interact with each other and give me specific input for revisions of the mission, vision, and strategic academic plan for the school. It's very effective." A president described the advisory council as assisting in the "environmental scan for strategic planning" and an engineering dean said that the council helps identify new technologies and business practices on the horizon, thus guiding the school's strategic planning.

Some presidents and deans mentioned the value of council advice on administrative operations, such as career services and information systems. One dean described the advisory council as providing unpaid "organizational consulting," while one president wrote that the advisory council has expanded connections for the institution's investment managers. Others emphasized that the council should advise on strategic questions and not become focused on management or financial matters.

The survey asked deans if their advisory councils play a role in the accreditation process for their schools or programs. The responses varied depending on the field. The majority of deans of arts and sciences said their councils do not play such a role, while the majority of business or management school and engineering school deans said that they do. Among the business schools, the advisory council participates in the accreditation process at 74 percent of public and at 61 percent of independent institutions; for engineering schools, the figures are 69 percent public and 53 percent independent.

---

6   The Fuqua School of Business at Duke University, "Board of Visitors," *http://www.fuqua.duke.edu/admin/corporaterelations/bov.htm* (accessed May 28, 2006).

Some deans offered comments that helped explain the council's role in the accreditation process. One explained that while the accrediting body relevant to his school does not require the involvement of an advisory council per se, it does require that the school engage its constituencies to assess outcomes and provide feedback. The advisory council is one of those constituencies, thus "it would be difficult to demonstrate engagement of outside constituencies without [the council's involvement]." Some deans said their schoolwide councils, or selected members, may meet with the peer review team during the campus visit, but that's all. Others said that departmental and program-level advisory councils play a more significant role in the accreditation process, but again, the study did not delve into their work at that level.

COUNCILS AS AMBASSADORS. Presidents and deans in both independent and public institutions highly ranked their councils' value as a source of external relationships with individuals other than donors, including government officials, local community residents, and others. Some mentioned the importance of state relationships, while others emphasized corporate connections or alumni.

Several comments from presidents and deans emphasized the council's ambassador role. Some mentioned the geographic diversity of their councils, providing representation in different parts of the country. Some council members host events in their home cities when the president or dean visits, helping to increase the institution's visibility and providing a local authenticator for its cause. In other words, as one dean said, "council members help to strengthen the school's brand."

Many also mentioned nonfinancial resources that council members bring to the institution. They provide career counseling and job and internship opportunities for students. Some provide assistance on student projects. Others help recruit faculty or identify adjunct professors. One dean described the school's advisory council as a "speaker's bureau" for professors to draw on in the classroom. Another highlighted its role in arranging for equipment loans and gifts-in-kind from industry.

Some public university advisory councils are engaged in higher education advocacy in their states. For example, the Clemson University Board of Visitors, an advisory group appointed by the university president, engages in Legislative Day at the state capital. Its members "are advocates for the university in their communities and vocal supporters of public and private funding for higher education."[7]

COUNCILS AS INTERNAL ADVOCATES. Deans were much more likely than presidents to highly value their councils as a source of political leverage within the institution. What sort of "political leverage" might deans gain from their councils? One dean described the council simply as "helpful in communicating with the higher echelons of the university." Another offered a more detailed example:

> Our advisory board has taken leadership in two important areas. First, they have provided a strong voice for our campaign for a new science building. Second, they have donated funds and pressured our board of trustees to attend to faculty salaries and research support. Having former members of the advisory board now serving on the board of trustees means a good line of communication to the senior governing body.

21

---

7   Clemson University, "Board of Visitors at Clemson University," *http://www.clemson.edu/bov/* (accessed February 19, 2007).

Of course, using a school advisory council for such internal purposes involves some risk and requires careful judgment. Some presidents might be unreceptive to an attempt to mobilize outside advisors, some of whom may also be government officials or members of the institution's governing board, to influence the allocation of institutional resources or priorities. However, with the right partnership between the president and a dean, an advisory council can help mobilize resources and support that can benefit both the professional school and the university. For example, some engineering school advisory councils, representing leading companies in a state, have persuaded state officials to see the schools as a lure for industry and a strategy for economic development. Their voices as advocates may carry more impact than those of presidents and deans alone.

The Council's Role in Fundraising

THE IMPORTANCE OF THE GOVERNING BOARD'S GIVING is a well-accepted principle in fundraising. For trustees, it is an obligation derived from their overall fiduciary responsibility. Moreover, the board's example of support is essential to securing gifts from others. If those closest to the institution do not support it, why would others? If trustees are not among the most generous and enthusiastic of the institution's donors, who else will be?

The mission statements of many advisory boards and councils often address the fundraising topic but usually not explicitly. For example, some say that council members help "identify new sources of support," "help to build relationships with new friends," or "alert the dean or president to opportunities for new partnerships." Nevertheless, the value of the advisory council as individuals who will give and help with fundraising ranked among the top three in responses from all categories of respondents.

Still, the comments of presidents and deans reveal varied opinions about fundraising. One president said, "Make fundraising a requirement," but one independent university dean urged, "Do not ask for money. Get them engaged." Expressing a similar approach, another dean advised, "Don't use your meetings to beg for money. Members of our board have offered, without solicitation, to fund programs they deem to be important." An independent institution dean, however, emphasized the importance of making the fundraising expectation explicit, noting that "it is difficult to shift the culture from an advisory board to a fundraising board once it is established." A public institution dean disagreed, saying, "It is important to segregate fundraising from the role of an advisory board."

THE IMPORTANCE OF INVOLVEMENT. Decades ago, veteran fund-raisers David Dunlop and G.T. "Buck" Smith described a process for cultivating donors known in the fundraising field as the "Five-I's." They are: interest, information, involvement, identity, and investment.

According to this theory, an individual's relationship with an institution usually begins simply with *interest*. This interest may flow from a natural affiliation, as in the case of an alumnus or the parent of a student, or it may result from proximity to the campus, a relationship with the president, or some other source. Interest deepens as individuals gain more *information* about the college or university, its programs, and people—perhaps as a result of deliberate initiatives by the institution. The critical step in building the relationship is *involvement*. The individual may begin to attend campus events and eventually accept some role, such as service on a council or board. Involvement leads to the next stage, in which the individual comes to *identify* with the college or university. An individual who identifies with an institution comes to share its successes and problems, takes pride in its achievements, and begins to share responsibility for addressing its goals and concerns. They have crossed the boundary between outsiders and insiders and have become part of the institution's family. They come to "own" it. That kind of emotional involvement, according to the theory, leads to the fifth "I," *investment*—in other words, significant financial support.

Sophisticated college and fundraising programs are predicated on the Five-I's, even if implicitly. Indeed, major gift officers work deliberately at planning "moves," that is, initiatives to move individuals through the process from interest to investment. Most use tracking systems, often known as moves management. Unfortunately, "move" sounds manipulative for what is really just a natural process of cultivating relationships, but the term is well-entrenched in the advancement office vocabulary.

Involvement is the key step in the process, but not all kinds of involvement are equal. Certainly, social events have their place in fundraising. Positive contacts between presidents or deans and prospective donors, opportunities to recognize donors or celebrate the achievements of distinguished alumni are important, as shared experiences help strengthen relationships. However, it is substantive involvement that most likely leads an individual to become emotionally identified with the institution. Once people take some responsibility for the institution—once they begin to engage with its aspirations, opportunities, and problems—its interests and theirs begin to merge.

A few years ago, I outlined the Five-I's in a presentation to a group of university deans, which also included one of the university's major donors. Afterward, the donor shared, "It was interesting to hear how this works from a fund raiser's point of view. And as a donor, I can say that you're right!" He went on to explain, "After I joined the university board and attended several meetings, I found myself worrying about some of the issues it faced as I was driving home from the meeting. Most of them involved the need for more resources. I was talking about it to my wife at home one evening after a board meeting and she asked 'Well, what are you going to do about it?' It was a good question. I realized that the university's goals had become important to me and that I needed to take some action. That's when I decided to make my first major gift."

A sense of ownership and personal responsibility for the institution's future are the precursors to significant philanthropy. That explains why so many of the top donors to higher education institutions are members of the governing board. Still, not everyone can serve on the governing board, and some likely would prefer not to. Advisory boards and councils provide the avenue for more people to be involved with the substance of the institution. In that way, they may come to understand and share its interests and become motivated to support it in a substantial way. In addition to helping shape the institution and its future, advisory boards and councils also broaden and deepen participation by those who can help make that future a reality.

To *feel* involved, advisory council members must be involved. A constant diet of show-and-tell presentations on the institution's accomplishments may inform. They may even impress and entertain, but receiving information is not the same as being involved in substance. Being impressed with the achievements of the president, the dean, the faculty, or the institution is not the same as wrestling with its aspirations, goals, and issues and leaving with a sense of having made a real contribution. As one president said, "Don't spend a lot of time talking to them." A dean advised, "Make sure that you engage the board on real issues of importance. The more qualified the board members, the more they want to spend their time on significant matters on which they can help." Another dean echoed, "Make sure they have something real to do, or they will feel that you are wasting their time. Meetings should not be 'everything is wonderful' sessions." Several presidents and deans derided what they commonly called "dog and pony shows" and expressed, "Listen more than you talk. Remember that you have incredibly talented and accomplished human beings in the room. Tap into their experience, knowledge, and business relationships."

Creating an advisory board or council *only* with the hope of more giving is likely to disappoint. To really engage people requires not only asking for their wealth, but also for their wisdom. It requires not just informing them, but involving them as real partners in shaping the institution's future. Asking for advice cannot be just a tactic for securing financial support. People are too smart and too experienced to be fooled; the request for help must be sincere. Advice must be respected, considered, and sometimes taken. It turns out that in reality, wealth and wisdom usually come together, but it is not always easy to strike the balance. As one dean noted, "The challenge is following up on the advice the board gives. This isn't always easy given faculty governance." Nevertheless, as several presidents and deans suggested, respecting and considering advice is often enough: "Don't ignore the council. Always act on its advice, even if in a negative way. In other words, at least show respect for the suggestion and run it up the flag pole."

The Minimum Gift Debate

THE QUESTION OF WHETHER BOARDS SHOULD HAVE A POLICY establishing a minimum annual gift from members—or a minimum that each member should either "give or get"—elicits varied opinions. AGB conducted a study in 2004 in which only 33 percent of independent colleges and universities had a policy requiring a specific minimum gift from their trustees. The study asked chief advancement officers and the chairs of board advancement committees at institutions without such a policy for their views. Both groups came out about 50-50 on the question; that is, about half of the respondents favored having such a policy and about half did not.

The 2006 AGB survey asked presidents and deans whether their advisory councils have policies requiring members to make a minimum annual gift. As shown in Table 2.1, most do not; of those who do, a gift between $1,000 and $5,000 is the most common standard.

On one side of the minimum gift argument, some people say that having a minimum ensures 100 percent board participation and gives board members and prospective members a clear sense of the financial expectations that accompany board membership. The other side argues that uniform expectations is a problem. Board members who are able to give much more may feel they have "paid their dues" by giving the minimum, leaving significant money on the table as a result.

TABLE 2.1 Policies on Minimum Annual Gifts

	President responses	Dean responses
No minimum gift required	78%	73%
Minimum gift less than $1,000	1%	7%
Minimum gift $1,000–4,999	19%	16%
Minimum gift $5,000–9,999	1%	2%
Minimum gift $10,000–24,999	0%	1%
Minimum gift $25,000+	0%	1%

Another argument against a minimum gift requirement for governing boards is the need to ensure such boards have a diverse membership. For example, it may be desirable to include recent alumni, community residents, teachers, or public servants on the governing board, so their perspectives can influence the institution's policies and programs. However,

24

many people in those categories may be unable to give more than a token gift. The dilemma then becomes whether to set a minimum so low that anyone can reach it or to make exceptions for individuals known not to possess financial means. The former approach increases the risk of giving less than the potential while the latter may result in a perception of two classes of trustees based on financial capability.

These arguments also have relevance to advisory boards and councils but with a few twists. It could be argued that diversity of membership on an advisory council is less important than on a governing board. Does a council really need diverse membership if it is not responsible for the institution's policies and programs? Are recent alumni, community residents, teachers, public servants, or others who may not be affluent really needed as members of such a council? Why not confine its membership to individuals who can give at a significant level and establish a minimum gift policy at that level?

First, there is the "money left on the table" argument. Even in a group of affluent people, some will be more affluent than others, and a minimum that accommodates all may lower the sights of those who could do more. Moreover, as the survey responses suggest, many value the advice their councils provide as much as they do the potential for increased financial support. That calls for the same diversity of backgrounds, experience, and financial situations as may be found on the governing board. There is also the council member's desire for "something different," discussed earlier in this chapter. Would a council of billionaires find it consistently stimulating to be in the company of others just like them, or is some diversity in the council membership essential to providing members a rewarding and enriching experience?

In view of such concerns, some experts recommend an approach that, despite its Marxist overtones, may be a good one: "From each according to his (or her) ability." In other words, one standard that can be applied across any board, however diverse its membership, is that members give in proportion to their financial capacity.

The debate on giving requirements is likely to continue. Survey respondents agree, however, that council members should receive clear expectations for giving and participating in fundraising when they join the council and throughout their terms of service. Ambiguity about the subject is likely to lead to misunderstandings and disappointment on all sides.

Clarity of Purposes

GOVERNING BOARD ROLES are defined by their legal obligations—the duties of care, loyalty, and obedience—and functions that are thoroughly articulated in the extensive governance literature. They hire the president, approve the budget, oversee management of the endowment, and approve the institution's programs, among other critical actions.

Advisory boards and councils, however, lack such clearly defined responsibilities and vary widely in their roles, holding the potential to disappoint their members; frustrate the expectations that presidents, chancellors, and deans hold for them; and complicate relationships and tensions inherent in higher education institutions. Clarity and openness about the advisory council's purpose was the single most common point of advice offered by the survey's presidents and deans.

Clarity is essential to prevent the council from overstepping its boundaries and encroaching on the responsibilities of the governing board or administration. As one dean wrote, "The council provides advice but should not expect to manage the college." Another warned, "Be sure you spell out the duties very carefully or they may wish to expand their... influence."

25

It is best to clearly state the council's purpose when it is established and to select initial members with those purposes in mind. It may be difficult to redirect a council if other priorities become more central later on. For example, many deans have convened councils for advice on curricular matters or help in job placement of students, and they recruit members to meet those goals. If the original purpose was program advice, the members may be academic or professional colleagues; likewise, a council focused on student career advising may include human resource officers of nearby corporations. If a subsequent dean decides that the council should shift to a fundraising mission, he or she may find the existing membership is not equipped to provide assistance. It may prove difficult to change the culture of an established council and make it effective with a different, new purpose in mind. One dean offered an example: "I inherited my board, and it is not a fundraising board. It is helpful in maintaining corporate contacts, but it is time-consuming for little financial benefit. If I had it to do over again, I would make it a fundraising board."

The purposes of the council must be restated and reinforced as membership changes and time passes. New member recruitment should include a forthright discussion of the council's purposes and responsibilities as well as the limitations on its authority and activity. Otherwise, the council's understanding of its role may drift over time, and new generations of members may inappropriately lead the council in directions not envisioned by its founders. One dean who responded to the survey emphasized this point: "We read their mission and purpose statement at the beginning of every meeting, which helps them remember their role."

Questions for Presidents, Chancellors, and Deans

- Are the purposes of your advisory board or council clear to you and to its members?

- How might the advisory council be more useful as an advocate for your institution, both internally and externally?

- Do members of your advisory board or council give personally and participate in fundraising from others?

- Have you communicated clear expectations about giving to council members when enlisted and periodically during their service?

EXHIBIT 2.0 Example of Council Mission Statement: Independent Institution

Methodist University Board of Visitors

1) To serve as an advisory council to the faculty, staff, president and Board of Trustees.

2) To be informed citizens about the structure and operations of the College and to serve as goodwill ambassadors for the College in the community.

3) To assist the College in developing financial resources through both identification and introduction of friends of the College.

4) To assist in identifying and recruiting students in specific geographical areas.

5) To provide the College with lecturers, community symposia, presentations, and/or demonstrations in various fields of expertise.

6) To provide advice for and assistance in enhancing the image and credibility of the College among a broader constituency.

Source: Methodist University, "Board of Visitors," *http://www.methodist.edu/Alum_dev/dev_vboard.htm* (accessed January 22, 2007).

EXHIBIT 2.1 Example of Council Mission Statement: Public Institution

University of Texas at Austin, McCombs School of Business Advisory Council

The advisory council will achieve its mission through a membership of diverse individuals whose stature and accomplishments bring credit to the school and who individually and collectively: engage in, assist, and support the fundraising efforts of the school; provide advice and counsel to the dean, faculty, and staff on strategy, important issues affecting the future of the school, curricula and programs, and external affairs; provide insights to the dean, faculty, and staff on how the school can enhance the impact of its services on various stakeholder groups; provide valuable contacts for faculty to provide access to the business community for research purposes, to increase the impact of their work on the business community, to inform their research and teaching, and to help them further develop their research, teaching, and public service skills; provide valuable contacts for students and advice in their career selection decisions and job-seeking activities; and provide input to the dean, faculty, and staff for assessing the progress of the school and charting future courses.

Source: McCombs School of Business, "Advisory Council Mission," *http://www.mccombs.utexas.edu/dean/advisory_council/mission.asp* (accessed January 22, 2007).

EXHIBIT 2.2 Example of Council Responsibilities: Independent Institution, Professional School

> **Claremont Graduate University, the Peter F. Drucker and Masatoshi Ito Graduate School of Management Board of Visitors**
>
> Roles and Responsibilities
>
> - Remain current with the Drucker School's priorities and programs
> - Participate in Claremont Graduate University and Drucker School related events
> - Assist in providing referrals for student internships and jobs for graduating students
> - Assist in cultivation and stewardship programs for potential donors and partners
> - Attend board meetings regularly
>
> *Source:* Claremont Graduate University, "Board of Visitors," *http://www.cgu.edu/pages/294.asp* (accessed February 14, 2007).

EXHIBIT 2.3 Example of Council Responsibilities: Independent Institution, Law School

> **Columbia University Law School**
>
> The board's principal responsibilities are:
>
> - To receive and consider information concerning the activities of the school and issues relating to legal education;
> - To counsel the dean and the faculty about the school's educational opportunities and directions;
> - To bring to the dean's attention new issues and concerns;
> - To inform the president and trustees about the state of the school and its needs;
> - To serve as liaison between the school and its graduates and friends by studying and communicating developments at the school.
>
> *Source:* Columbia Law School, "Board of Visitors," *http://www.law.columbia.edu/alumni/bov* (accessed February 14, 2007).

CHAPTER 3

Organizing and Managing Advisory Boards and Councils

I**N THIS CHAPTER,** we look at the nuts and bolts of advisory boards and councils to see who serves on them, how the groups are organized, and how they are managed. The information comes from responses by presidents and deans to the AGB survey. While the survey covered many boards and councils, there may be other variations that are not included in this discussion. It is also important to remember that survey responses describe what is done, but not necessarily what is "best practice." Indeed, it would be difficult to define what is "best," as advisory councils serve the particular needs of their institutions and reflect the different traditions and realities of each campus. Moreover, presidents and deans who participated in the survey vary in how they organize and manage advisory boards and councils. Despite the lack of consensus, this chapter will discuss some of the pros and cons of the different approaches.

Bylaws, Guidelines, and Job Descriptions

T**HE SURVEY ASKED PRESIDENTS AND DEANS** whether their advisory groups have formal bylaws or job descriptions, which some call a mission statement, statement of purpose, or guidelines. The intention was to learn whether councils have formal structures or exist as informal groups. Most councils have either bylaws or at least formal job descriptions or guidelines that define how the council is structured and operates, although about one-third have neither. There were no significant differences among responses by deans of arts and sciences, business, and engineering except that advisory councils at colleges of arts and sciences in private universities are somewhat less likely to have formal bylaws or descriptions than others.

Advisory council bylaws typically outline the council's purpose, size, method of appointing or electing members, and terms of service. Some identify council officers, their method of appointment or election, and their leadership terms of service. If the council has committees, their purposes and missions also are described. Most bylaws specify the number of meetings, who can call them, and requirements about attendance, meeting minutes, and other operational procedures. Bylaws also stipulate amendment procedures.

Bylaws are documents usually developed by the board of an incorporated organization, pursuant to a charter. Advisory

TABLE 3.0 Do Councils Have Bylaws and Job Descriptions?

	President responses	Dean responses
Bylaws	31%	38%
Formal job description, but not bylaws	31%	20%
Bylaws and formal job description	5%	6%
Neither (informal)	33%	36%

councils that are informal do not require formal bylaws. Indeed, there may be a risk that having bylaws will imply the council has more standing and authority than it does. However, it is good practice to have at least some written description of the council's procedures, even if it does not take the form of official bylaws. A single page may be adequate. For example, Appendix I includes a description of Whittier College's Poet Council, which covers the same points as more formal bylaws—the council's size, membership composition, method of selection, and terms of service.

Some public universities and their colleges and schools are required to have formal bylaws for their advisory councils. For example, the Rules and Regulations of the board of regents of the University of Texas System requires that "Subject to the approval of the president of the institution, each advisory council shall adopt bylaws for its internal governance that are consistent with this [rule] and that substantially comply with the model bylaws developed by the Office of General Counsel."[1] (See Appendix I for the complete model bylaws.) The regents' Rules allow individual institutions to determine council size and terms of service, but they clearly state that councils report to the dean and ultimately the institution's president. They also clarify that advisory councils are a part of the university, not separate legal entities, with no governing authority. The Texas model bylaws also emphasize the council's role in securing private support, include a conflict of interest policy, and define the vice chancellor for external affairs' role in coordinating council rosters.

Presidents and deans responding to the AGB survey offered varied opinions on whether or not councils should have formal bylaws or job descriptions. Most recognized the need for clearly defining the council's purposes and the roles and expectations of its members, but not all favored having written documents. Some preferred flexibility, like one dean who wrote:

> An advisory council should exist to help the dean. If the dean feels it is not helpful, then the dean should change it so that it is helpful. We used to have bylaws and they were very rigid—Roberts Rules of Order were observed and so on. I removed all of that and basically use the council for advice and ideas. Then we have lunch. It works well.

Another dean suggested that among a new dean's first actions should be to dissolve his or her predecessor's advisory council and start over. Although the respondent did not provide further explanation, one can assume that he does not favor much formality about the council; it serves at the pleasure of the dean.

Advisory Council Membership

HOW BIG ARE MOST ADVISORY COUNCILS? The most common size of advisory councils, in both the independent and public sector, is between 11 and 30 members, with well over one-half of all councils falling in that range. That is true for both councils that serve an entire institution and those related to an individual college or school within the university. Nevertheless, council size varied widely with 5 percent having 50 or more members. Comments from survey respondents indicated there is no consensus on what is the appropriate size. It may depend on the purposes envisioned for the council.

Governing board size has been a subject of discussion in recent years. Some experts argue that large boards may inhibit participation and adversely affect governance. In a room

---

1   The University of Texas System, *Rules and Regulations of the Board of Regents*, Series 60302, Section 4.1.

of 50 people, some may remain silent or passive, assuming that somebody else will handle the matter at hand. Some people may be reluctant to challenge the president or other board members before a large group, perhaps out of courtesy or fear of embarrassment. In sum, a large board can turn into an audience rather than an interactive and engaged group. Indeed, the relatively large size of the governing board has been mentioned as a contributing factor in some widely publicized cases of board failure at universities and nonprofit organizations in recent years.

Advisory councils do not have the same responsibilities as governing boards; therefore, having a large group may not be problematic. For example, if one purpose of the council is to involve more people to become advocates and donors or to evaluate individuals to serve on the governing board, then a large-sized council may be advantageous. On the other hand, making the advisory council too large may lead to a meeting format that is low on discussion and high on show-and-tell. That experience is not likely to attract strong council members or keep them involved for long. The other reality is that individuals most likely will perceive a large council as less prestigious than one that is more selective, making it less attractive to high-level individuals the institution wants to recruit. To paraphrase Mark Twain, who wants to belong to a club that everybody—or almost everybody—can join? With a large council, it may be necessary to organize committees to provide opportunities for discussion, but the management of the council then becomes a greater task. Meanwhile, full council meetings may become back-to-back committee reports and still keep members from meaningful discussion.

The AGB survey found some presidents and deans favor a small council. One president advised "start small" and add new members "carefully" over time. Another recommended keeping the membership at no more than 10 to 15 individuals to facilitate discussion. One dean described a recent restructuring that reduced the advisory council from 60 to 30 members: "Previously, the council was a show-and-tell operation. Now members are fully engaged and energized." Still, not all agreed. One noted that members may be less diligent about attending advisory council meetings than governing or foundation board meetings with legal responsibilities, so a larger advisory council may be necessary to ensure a critical mass of attendees.

TABLE 3.1 Size of Advisory Councils

Number of members	President responses	Dean responses
1–10	7%	13%
11–20	27%	42%
21–30	26%	25%
31–40	25%	9%
41–50	10%	6%
>50	5%	5%

One of the larger advisory councils reported in the survey is the University of Texas at Austin Engineering Advisory Board, a group 100-strong that includes alumni, nonalumni donors, community leaders, and corporate executives from various industries. They assist with fundraising, provide guidance in teaching and research, and serve as advocates for the school. Dean Ben Streetman reports the size of the council is an advantage, because it provides the School of Engineering with the opportunity to involve a wide range of influential alumni and friends.[2]

2   Ben D. Streetman, personal communication with author, March 5, 2007.

WHO SERVES ON COUNCILS? Constituencies represented on advisory councils are similar in both independent and public institutions as well as on councils serving entire campuses and those affiliated with a specific academic unit. Not surprisingly, alumni serve on the overwhelming majority of councils, but it is important to emphasize these groups are not alumni association boards. As one president explained, alumni serve on the advisory council as individuals; they are not there to represent the interests of alumni or the alumni association. Other groups frequently represented on councils are donors who are not alumni, corporate executives, and local community leaders. Public university presidents were more likely than their independent counterparts to report state government officials, faculty, and students serve on their advisory councils. More than one-half of the councils described by independent institution presidents include parents of students, who form an important constituency for tuition-dependent colleges and universities.

TABLE 3.2 Who Serves on Advisory Councils

	President responses	Dean responses
Alumni	85%	94%
Donors and prospects, other than alumni	86%	77%
Corporate executives	87%	90%
Academics from other institutions	17%	20%
Members of the institution's governing board	26%	23%
Local government officials	32%	20%
Local community leaders	68%	57%
Parents	44%	15%
Other	14%	14%

Some presidents and deans suggested the need to balance council membership among constituencies and generations. One described how the school's council chair was a retired individual with time to devote to its activities. The council at this school includes nonalumni and alumni of all ages. As the dean describes, "Older alumni lend influence and contribute financially to the university; younger alumni plan and organize events and help in a more hands-on way. That seems to work."

One individual suggested the importance of having faculty serve on advisory boards and councils, as faculty control the curriculum and should have opportunities to hear curricular concerns or suggestions directly from council members. Having faculty on the advisory council might also help allay their suspicion, if any, about the council's work.

Although the AGB study did not explicitly ask about faculty inclusion on councils, a handful of presidents and deans did list faculty and/or student members in their comments under the "Other" category. Many presidents and deans emphasized the importance of having faculty and students interact with the advisory council and participate in its meetings on appropriate occasions. Chapter 4 includes a discussion of how faculty and students participate in council activities and the importance of including them in at least some council meetings and events. That said, there are also good reasons not to include faculty as council members. Doing so could inhibit frank discussion between presidents or deans and their advisory councils, weakening the council's sounding board role they value. Having faculty members involved in every council discussion also could result in too much focus on internal matters, including curriculum, and detract from their advising on broad strategic issues and building external relationships.

HOW ARE COUNCIL MEMBERS SELECTED? The AGB survey asked presidents and deans to describe how they identify and formally elect or appoint new members to their advisory councils. Their responses indicated that recommendations for new council members come from several sources—most commonly the advisory council itself, the president or dean whom that council advises, and the advancement or development office of the institution, college, or school. More than one-half of the deans also mentioned faculty as a source of suggestions, but fewer than a quarter of presidents indicated that faculty provide names.

Table 3.3 summarizes responses on how council members are formally elected or appointed to serve. They suggest that most councils "belong" to the president or dean whom they advise, with that president or dean making appointments to the group in almost two-thirds of all cases. The second most common pattern is the self-perpetuating council; that is, the council selects its own members. Other responses reveal a variety of methods for selecting council members.

TABLE 3.3 How Council Members Are Elected or Appointed to Serve

	President responses	Dean responses
Appointed by the president or dean it advises	62%	60%
Appointed by president/chancellor (deans' councils only)	NA	8%
Council elects its own members	13%	10%
Elected by another group (for example, alumni association, foundation)	5%	1%
Informal—no set method	2%	3%
A mix of the above	9%	10%
Other responses	9%	8%

Although both presidents and deans identified the advancement or development office as one of the most common sources of names for their councils, the advancement office generally does not select the council. In fact, only four presidents indicated the advancement office selects members of their advisory council. Of course, where the council may exist informally without bylaws, the distinction between identifying potential new members and appointing them may, in practice, be negligible.

When asked about college or school advisory councils, 8 percent of deans indicated the president or chancellor appoints the members. However, the deans' comments revealed a variety of actual situations. Several reported that presidents formally make the appointment upon the dean's recommendation. In at least one case, the dean's nomination requires approval from both the president and the governing board. Others reported the dean nominates new members to the advisory council, which then elects them, and some observed the council's approval is generally pro forma. As one dean described, "Technically, the council elects its own new members, but I am heavily involved in shaping the nominees." Some deans described a process of joint appointment, that is, the dean and the council chair or the dean and president jointly appoint new council members.

The views on the dean's and the president's or chancellor's role in appointing members to college and school councils vary. Having presidential appointments, or even confirmation by the governing board, may give the council a special legitimacy, enhance its prestige, and increase the perception of the council as a farm club for the governing board. However, some deans might worry that an advisory council so appointed might come to see itself as responsible to the president or the governing board, or even see itself as representing the university's interests or evaluating the school or dean on the president's behalf. Also, if the dean's appointment of council members is approved by the president and/or the governing board, does the dean have the authority to remove them if they do not participate as hoped or negatively influence the council? Having clear, written guidelines helps clarify such points and avoid potentially difficult situations.

The AGB survey did not ask deans to express a view specifically on the method of council selection, although a few comments addressed it obliquely. For example, one dean encouraged colleagues to "work closely with the president and the advancement office, but try to keep the dean's office the central contact point." It is likely that deans' opinions on the best method for selecting their advisory councils would vary considerably, depending on the personal and political dynamics at their individual institutions.

Several presidents and deans mentioned the need to choose advisory council members with care. One president urged, "Get the right people on the bus," while another cautioned, "Be sure to pick the right people or it will be a never-ending source of trouble." One dean advised beginning a new council with a core of alumni members, who will be among the most committed, then expanding to include other advisors with expertise in areas of growth for the school. Another advised deans to devote more time and attention to developing strong relationships with a small council rather than devoting "too much energy to convincing others to join."

Regardless of the advancement office's role in identifying or selecting council members, there should be a central clearinghouse for prospective members of dean-level advisory councils. The advancement office, which manages the clearance of fundraising prospects, is likely to have the most comprehensive data and be best prepared to coordinate this process. Proceeding with an appointment to a council without clearance through some institution-wide system can be risky. First, the university could be embarrassed by the appointment of an individual who has a conflict of interest or some other relationship with another part of the institution that the college or school is not aware of. Furthermore, multiple invitations to serve may have the same result as multiple solicitations for gifts. At the least, the individual may be annoyed and perceive the university as disorganized and mismanaged; at the worst, the individual may give less total time and money than might have been possible with a more coordinated approach. Finally, uncoordinated recruiting affects the university's relationship with corporations and other organizations. For example, there is a clear hierarchy and sociology within most corporations, so if a midlevel corporate executive is serving on one advisory council at a university, it may be difficult to recruit another, more senior executive from the same company, even if it is for a different council at another of the university's schools. Ultimately, universities must use a coordinated approach to ensure the right people are involved in the right roles.

Advisory Council Operations and Structure

THE COUNCIL CHAIR. MOST ADVISORY COUNCILS, including 64 percent reported by presidents and 73 percent by deans, have a chair. The president or dean appoints about one-half of those chairs, while the council itself elects about one-third. The rest are selected through various other methods.

Some presidents and deans emphasized the importance of the council chair appointment. As one wrote, "The chair of the council makes a significant difference in determining its effectiveness." Another recommended having term limits or some other system for rotating chairs or using cochairs to distribute leadership responsibility. Several observed that the president's or dean's relationship with the chair is central to a successful relationship with the entire council.

TABLE 3.4 **Method for Selecting Advisory Council Chair of Those Who Have a Chair**

	President responses	Dean responses
Appointed by the president, chancellor, dean	50%	49%
Elected by the council	33%	35%
Selected by the advancement office	6%	0
Flexible, happens in different ways	4%	6%
Other	6%	10%

Having the right chair sets the tone for the council. In other words, a prominent and respected leader can make council membership attractive to others of similar stature. An effective chair also can serve as a buffer between the president or dean and members of the council, raising sensitive issues—for example, the need to provide financial support—more effectively than the president or dean. Because chairs can address council members as a peer, or as a leader, they can pursue the council's agenda and goals for the university, college, or school without appearing self-serving.

TERMS OF SERVICE. The AGB survey found most advisory councils do not have formal limits on the terms that individuals can serve. Only 36 percent of those identified by presidents and 38 percent of those identified by the deans have such limits. Of those that do have fixed terms, they are typically two or three years and permit members to serve two or three terms before stepping down from the council. In many cases, terms are flexible, depending primarily on the pleasure of the president or dean. As one dean wrote, "Terms are fuzzy but not indefinite." Also, judging by the comments of some deans and presidents, some councils with fixed terms and/or term limits make exceptions or do not rigidly enforce those limits for members they want to keep involved.

There are, of course, pros and cons to such flexibility. Indeed, the subject of term limits draws almost as much debate as the question of minimum gift requirements. On the one hand, because advisory groups are not governing boards, there may be less concern about the need to periodically refresh the membership. One concern about governing boards that do not limit terms is that long-serving members may become quiescent and cease to question the administration about key policies. "Country club boards," where members have known each other a long time and have developed a passive style in their interactions with the president, have been implicated in several well-publicized governance failures. In contrast, advisory boards do not share the governing board's fiduciary responsibility; they advise and assist the president or dean. Thus, some might question the need for fixed terms or limits on service; individuals should serve as long as the president or dean values their involvement and contribution.

On the other hand, without term limits council members eventually could lose interest and cease to attend meetings. The dean or president might have the authority to drop people who do not participate but that may involve embarrassing or offending an ally of the university. Consequently, a number of inactive members may continue to appear on council rosters out of courtesy. Rather than remove inactive members, a president or dean might try to re-energize the group by adding new people, making the council larger. With this approach, however, new members might begin to question why their colleagues are failing to participate. They might then view the council as unimportant or just "honorary." A council carrying the dead weight of absent members may lose its energy and cease to attract individuals who could serve the university well.

That said, some advancement officers have concerns about term limits, arguing that cultivating relationships takes time. Term limits may force individuals off the council just when their interest is at its peak and they are ready to make a major gift. During their absence from the board or council, their interests could turn elsewhere. It would be better, then, for presidents and deans to have the ability to reappoint council members as long as it is beneficial to do so, whether because of their sound advice or because of their potential to make a major gift. Then again, not reappointing may be a decision that many presidents and deans find difficult to make. In the case of a governing board, the failure to reelect a nonperforming member is a decision for which the full board holds responsibility. It is a more difficult decision for a president or dean to reach alone—it's just more personal—and without term limits the advisory council may be diminished in ways discussed above.

COMMITTEES. Some advisory councils operate as a whole, while others have committees with specific responsibilities. Dividing council work among committees may provide opportunities for discussion and hands-on work, especially if the full council is large.

As an example of committee structures, the National Engineering Advisory Council at Marquette University has three committees organized around three functions consistent with the council's mission: building bridges to business, building bridges to the university, and providing advice to the college. Descriptions of the committees include suggestions of possible activities in which they may engage. The bylaws of the Advisory Council for the College of Social Sciences and Public Affairs at Boise State University also include descriptions of four standing committees, called "teams," along with a statement of each committee's charge. Finally, the Columbia Law School Board of Visitors has three committees, some accomplishments of which are noted on the school's Web site.[3]

---

3   See *http://www.law.columbia.edu/alumni/bov/committee* (accessed February 2007)

EXHIBIT 3.0 Example of Advisory Council Committees (Independent Institution)

Marquette University • College of Engineering • National Advisory Council

COMMITTEE STRUCTURE

The Council will have three working committees: Building Bridges to Business, Building Bridges to the University and Advisory Support to the COE. The chairs of the three working committees will be appointed by the Council Chair in consultation with the Dean.

Building Bridges to Business

MISSION

To gain access to local and national industry for the purpose of providing input to the College regarding technology and business trends that should be considered for program and curriculum development. The Committee will be responsible for identifying opportunities for collaboration between the COE and Business, such as co-op sites, tours, internships, mentors, speakers etc.

Possible Activities

- Link faculty researchers with industrial research opportunities.
- Volunteer or recruit graduate engineer volunteers to speak to freshman Engineering classes on careers and other work/life perspectives.
- Offer to lecture to a class on your specialty area. If distance is a barrier, arrange for a teleconference call, a Web cast, or a videoconference.

Building Bridges to the University

MISSION

To enhance the reputation of the college by seeking feedback from the university in a proactive way on a regular basis.

POSSIBLE ACTIVITIES

- Set up a face to face meeting with the Provost to share information regarding the activities of the NAC and the COE.
- Engage the administration in using different language regarding COE scholarships and engineering practices.
- Form strategic connections with other deans and colleges to share best practices.
- Create opportunities and build relationships with key university personnel.

Advisory Support to the College of Engineering

MISSION

To provide direction and guidance to the college regarding its strategic plan, recruitment of students, and academic matters.

POSSIBLE ACTIVITIES

- Prepare a list of college of engineering competitors.
- Develop a set of metrics for the College to use in bench marking it's programs and practices.

Source: http://www.marquette.edu/eng/pages/GettingInvolved/advisory.html (accessed February 2007).

EXHIBIT 3.1 **Example of Advisory Council Standing Committees (Public Institution)**

38

Boise State University • College of Social Sciences and Public Affairs • Advisory Council

Teams of the Council

1. Community Relations Team:

This team is charged with promoting the mission of the SSPA College in the community, and throughout the state, when appropriate. This task includes using the Council's networks to identify opportunities and emerging needs in the community and state. The Council will take actions to increase opinion leaders' and the public's awareness, understanding, and interaction with the College's mission, research, educational programs, institutes, and centers.

2. Fundraising Team:

This team is charged with fulfilling the SSPAAC's purpose of assisting the College to increase revenues. This task includes fundraising, grants, in-kind contributions, federal, state legislative, and Board of Education financial support, and other potential sources of revenues.

3. Faculty and Student Support Team:

This team is charged with assisting the SSPA College in attracting and retaining outstanding, energetic faculty. This undertaking includes providing incentives and supporting faculty research, recognizing outstanding teaching, as well as enhancing faculty involvement with the community in their respective fields. Council members could facilitate positions on boards, advisory participation with community organizations and agencies, as guest speakers, experts, etc. The council could also assist in supporting student internship and research programs.

4. Executive Team:

[DRAFT] This team is charged with general administrative and strategic planning issues of the SSPAAC. This task includes needs assessment and changes where appropriate. The executive team shall approve all chair appointments to various teams and retain the right to appoint ad hoc teams and task forces as they see fit. The executive team shall consist of the dean, the president, the president-elect, the former president, and the chairs of the standing teams.

This team is also charged with soliciting and recommending new/replacement members to the Council. The team shall make every effort to make sure that the membership represents the diverse nature of the region (both individually and by professional affiliation). The team shall recommend new/replacement member to the entire Council for approval.

Source: http://sspa.boisestate.edu/3bylaws_sspa.html (accessed February 2007).

**EXHIBIT 3.2 Example of Committees
(Independent Institution, Professional School)**

Columbia Law School • Board of Visitors

STEERING COMMITTEE

The Steering Committee suggests agenda items for the Board of Visitors' meetings. The goal is to make meetings valuable and productive for both BOV members and for Columbia Law School. In addition, the Steering Committee is charged with identifying promising initiatives for the Law School. Thus far, the Steering Committee has created three subcommittees focused on students, facilities and financial aid, and faculty. The students subcommittee created a survey in 2003 which was distributed to all Board members. The results of this survey have been distributed to various administrative offices at the Law School with the hope of involving Board members in more Law School activities.

INTERNATIONAL COMMITTEE

The International Committee concentrates on a wide range of international issues. Some of these include admissions, placement, orientation of incoming students, and the steps necessary for Columbia Law School to remain competitive as an educational environment for international students. There are issues regarding the internationalization of the student body, programs, and curriculum that the group will consider by working with the Faculty International Law Task Force.

RECENT GRADUATES COMMITTEE

The Recent Graduates Committee was formed to focus on the relationship between Columbia Law School and its recent graduates. The Committee will look at the services which the Law School provides to its alumni and also at how the Law School can better serve this constituency. The group will consider several programs at the Law School including the "Buddy Program" which will provide students with mentors, the proposed online directory of graduates, and career services for graduates.

Source: http://www.law.columbia.edu/alumni/bov/committees (accessed February, 2007).

Some experts today advise governing boards to limit the number of committees to those that are essential to the board's work. They offer two principal arguments. First, having too many committees may turn full board meetings into a parade of committee reports, leaving little time for the full board to discuss important issues. Second, if committees are organized along the same lines as executive portfolios—for example, development, student affairs, finance, and so forth—the structure may inevitably drive the board down into management silos, distracting them from the big-picture issues on which they should focus. Instead of having several standing board committees, many experts advocate using task forces to address key issues or problems coming before the board. Much like presidential search committees, these task forces have a specific assignment and are dissolved when they complete it.

Organizing standing committees of an advisory board or council raises an additional issue of costs in time, effort, and resources. Governing board committees are usually staffed by executives of the institution, often vice presidents. For example, the vice president for advancement staffs the board's committee on advancement, the vice president for student affairs supports the student affairs committee, and the financial vice president works closely with the committee on financial affairs. Their offices support the committee's work, preparing materials, working with the committee chair to develop the meeting agenda, and managing communication with committee members between formal meetings. As one dean cautioned, the advisory council is usually an add-on to an already "bulky portfolio." Breaking the council into committees can multiply the administrative support required. Will committee appointments need to be communicated? Membership lists maintained? Agendas developed, meeting rooms booked, and minutes prepared for every committee meeting in addition to meetings of the full advisory council? These tasks can require significant staff resources that may not be readily available within an academic unit.

Councils should not form committees unless there is a clear definition of the purposes and work they will pursue. The ratio of benefits to costs also should be considered. As an alternative, task forces could be created to consider special topics or issues that require deliberation by a small group. One dean provided an example: "We use small working groups to consider specific issues, such as a new major or creation of a career advising center, then make recommendations to the entire council and eventually to the dean."

Questions for Presidents, Chancellors, and Deans

- Does your advisory board or council have written bylaws or other documents that detail such matters as purposes, membership criteria, council size, participation requirements, and terms of service?

- If your advisory council has committees, do they serve real needs and have meaningful work to do?

- Are you satisfied with the current procedure for identifying and appointing new council members?

CHAPTER 4

Working With the Advisory Board or Council

EFFECTIVE ADVISORY BOARDS AND COUNCILS don't just happen. It is not enough to identify a group of people and expect them to work well without the investment of time, effort, and money. Nor would it be realistic to think that relationships can be established and nurtured without a sustained commitment of those same resources and careful attention to ongoing communications. This chapter examines how presidents and deans work with their advisory boards and councils, including who provides staff and budget support, how often they meet, what kinds of activities and subjects comprise a council meeting, and how institutional leaders maintain communication and strengthen relationships with council members between meetings.

Supporting the Advisory Council's Work

AN ADVISORY COUNCIL REQUIRES MORE WORK than presidents or deans are likely to handle alone, given their other responsibilities and the many demands for their time and attention from both internal and external constituencies. Assigning a staff person to manage the advisory council program is essential, and as with council relations, ignoring individuals who accept this responsibility will likely lead to problems. The council's contributions also need budgetary support. Meetings may require materials, facilities, and perhaps expenses for meals and social activities. To gain insight on these issues, the survey asked presidents and deans about the source of staff and budgetary support for their council's activity and invited their advice on the subject.

STAFF SUPPORT. Presidents and deans differed in their responses regarding staff support. For advisory councils serving the entire institution, the advancement or development office provides support in 60 percent of cases; the individual who supports the governing board, for example, a board secretary, handles another 18 percent; while president's office staff, such as an executive assistant or assistant to the president, supports the remaining 22 percent.

      Deans, however, reported their councils receive staff support from a person on their staff in 71 percent of the responses. The advancement office of the particular college or school provides the support for another 15 percent; the central university advancement office, the president's office, or someone in the governing board office covers the rest. One of the deans emphasized that deans themselves support the advisory council with assistance from the advancement office or another staff member.

BUDGET FOR THE COUNCIL. In addition to staff, advisory council programs require adequate budgetary support. Six percent of presidents and 11 percent of deans indicated their councils are "self-supporting," but their comments offered further clarification. In most cases, council members cover their own travel expenses to the meetings, while the institution covers the costs of the meeting itself, including facilities rental, materials, some meals, and some social activities. If council members travel from out of town, they often pay the costs of their own lodging; although in some instances, the institution pays.

The most common budget source is the president's office (53 percent of presidents) or the dean's office (73 percent of deans). Thirty-five percent of presidents funded their councils through the advancement office, but only 6 percent of deans said their college or school advancement office funds their advisory council. Other sources of council support include gifts, corporate funds, and—in the case of one fortunate dean—income from the dean's endowed chair.

Council Meetings

MOST ADVISORY COUNCILS MEET TWICE EACH YEAR; that is the case for 48 percent of those reported by presidents and 59 percent reported by deans. The next most frequent pattern (34 percent of presidents and 26 percent of deans) is for the council to meet three or four times each year. A relatively small number of councils meet only once a year or more than four times. Regardless of meeting frequency, presidents and deans stressed the importance of respecting council members' demanding business and personal schedules by holding meetings at convenient times for members and keeping them at a reasonable length.

Presidents and deans also emphasized that effective meetings have planned agendas rather than open-ended discussion. A discussion without an agenda is like a trip without a destination—it may lead nowhere or to a place that the president or dean would rather not go. Such informality also may suggest to the council that its work is neither substantive nor important.

One question presidents and deans often ask is what issues to bring before the advisory council and what mix of activities to include in their meetings. While meetings of governing boards, foundation boards, and alumni association boards also require planning, some of their agenda items are fixed and predictable. For example, discussing fundraising, setting tuition, receiving committee reports, approving faculty appointments and promotions, and other routine matters may consume a significant portion of the governing board's agenda. Furthermore, boards with legal responsibilities have business to conduct, and the agenda is often driven by the executive staff's need to inform the board or gain its approval. In contrast, the advisory council agenda may be more of a blank slate. Without formal actions to schedule, presidents or deans, their staff, and perhaps the council chair or other members must decide what topics and activities to include.

Table 4.0 shows survey responses of the types of activities that are "always" or "almost always" included in the council program.

TABLE 4.0 Advisory Council Meeting Activities

	Percentage reporting that activity is "always" or "almost always" included			
	Independent institution presidents	Public institution presidents	Independent institution deans	Public institution deans
Presentations about programs	81%	73%	62%	68%
Discussion of issues, priorities, plans	84%	100%	92%	93%
Discussion of curriculum	5%	7%	41%	29%
Discussion of fund-raising	44%	13%	38%	58%
Social activities	63%	60%	49%	57%

The responses suggest that the typical advisory council meeting is a blend of presentations, discussions, and social activities. Presentations and discussions about issues are always or almost always included in council meetings. Curriculum is less often discussed; not surprisingly, it is more commonly found in meetings of councils related to academic units than in institutionwide ones working with a president. Discussions about fundraising are not a part of council meetings as often as some people might assume, although most councils discuss fundraising at least "sometimes." It is interesting to observe that deans in public institutions ranked fundraising somewhat higher as a focus of their advisory council agendas than did their counterparts in the independent sector.

PRESENTATIONS. Most advisory council programs include presentations by the president or dean, other members of the executive staff, or faculty. For example, faculty may report on their research or provide insights on some current events. Advancement officers may report on progress in a campaign, while business officers may provide updates on plans for a new facility. Such presentations can be interesting and, as one dean expressed it, they "give something back to the council members" for their commitment of time and energy. Presentations and reports inform council members of the institution's goals and achievements. As they become knowledgeable about programs and research, they become better ambassadors and advocates for the university, college, or school.

However, as many survey respondents emphasized, too much show-and-tell (what several called "dog and pony shows") can be deadly. A steady diet of presentations—especially those that extol the institution's (or administration's) virtues and accomplishments—wastes council members' time and fails to satisfy their desire to contribute meaningfully to the institution. It also leads them to question whether the term "advisory" has any meaning or if the institution just wants to subject a captive audience to extended solicitations for support. Ultimately, this approach does not constitute the substantive involvement that builds the sense of ownership that may lead to substantial financial investment.

DISCUSSION OF ISSUES, PRIORITIES, PLANS. As their name implies, advisory councils consider and provide insight on important questions, issues, and plans for presidents and deans. However, identifying the right issues to bring before the advisory council requires careful judgment.

Although one president advised sharing "everything you show the board of trustees, except personnel matters," it might not be wise or appropriate to seek the advisory council's advice on sensitive matters under debate by the governing board. That could be risky if some members of the governing board are on the advisory council and carry the discussion back to the other body. The governing board might appreciate the additional input on the matter, or they might feel having other groups discuss the issue compromises their authority. It might be appropriate and useful for a school advisory council to discuss fundraising needs and priorities in preparation for a campaign, as their insights into prospective donors' perceptions could help shape the campaign's objectives. It would be inappropriate, however, for the council to debate alternative investment choices for the endowment, which is a responsibility of the governing or foundation board.

As one dean noted, receiving the council's advice on matters of curriculum or academic policy may be frustrating and counterproductive if the faculty does not share the council's view. The faculty oversees curriculum, and it has no obligation to accept contrary input from advisory council members. However, discussions that focus on the big picture—for example, necessary workforce skills for the future—may be more appropriate than considering specific program or course content.

One survey respondent dean wisely suggested that it may be best to bring big picture, "long-run" issues to the advisory council, rather than "trivial short-run" issues currently affecting the campus. For example, it might be appropriate for a business school advisory council to discuss the impact of technology on business practice but refrain from debating what elements should be included in the syllabus for a finance course.

What do councils discuss and on what matters do they provide advice? Deans and presidents offered examples:

- Our council discussions focus on certain themes, for example, diversity, undergraduate research, faculty development, facilities.
- The council discusses special projects, for example, plans for a new building.
- Our council advises us on relationships with the local school district and community colleges.
- For each meeting, we assign the council "homework" related to some higher education issue of importance to us.
- The council receives updates from the career services office and provides input on job placement and internship needs.

DISCUSSION OF FUNDRAISING AND PROSPECTS. Presidents and deans ranked fundraising among the advisory council's three most important purposes, and they indicated that fundraising goals and donor prospects are sometimes discussed at council meetings, although not on every occasion.

The data reveal some interesting patterns. Few public university presidents reported their advisory councils put fundraising on their agenda. At independent institutions, however, 11 percent of presidents said their council agendas always include fundraising, 34 percent said almost always, and 45 percent said sometimes. Of deans at public universities, 26 percent always include discussion of fundraising, 33 percent almost always, and 28 percent sometimes; at independent universities, 12 percent of deans reported always, 26 percent almost always, and 37 percent sometimes. In other words, dean's councils at public institutions are more likely to discuss fundraising at their meetings than their counterparts at independent universities. Perhaps this is because public university governing boards are less engaged in fundraising than those at independent institutions, making the advisory council more important in fundraising. Breaking down the results according to the academic disciplines or fields encompassed by the schools does not show any significant patterns.

In earlier decades, friend-raising and fundraising were not significant among the university dean's responsibilities. Deans were primarily academic leaders; they were of their faculties. With the exception of particularly entrepreneurial deans, external relations activities, such as fundraising, were left to the university president and the governing board. If colleges and schools did have advisory boards or councils, they were likely to be experts in an academic discipline who advised on program and curricular matters.

Today's world could not be more different. In most universities, both private and public, deans are expected to be deeply engaged in fundraising for their colleges or schools; indeed, many devote a significant and increasing amount of time to these activities. Most advertisements for open deanships now include fundraising experience among a candidate's sought-after qualities. University campaign goals often include component goals for individual units, and deans—together with unit-based advancement officers—share a significant responsibility for their attainment. The dean's role clearly has evolved from that of academic leader to more of a chief executive, engaged in the pursuit of both internal and external goals. The dean's role in American higher education over the past three decades has expanded concurrently with the increasing number and importance of advisory councils and their shift in purposes from advising on academic programs to facilitating and strengthening external relationships. Not surprisingly, the number of advancement or development professional staff working within specific academic units also has exploded. Today, most universities have unit-based advancement staff in major colleges and schools, including some academic departments, research centers, and other subunits. In some cases, individual advancement officers support the deans in their fundraising activity, but larger units may have an advancement staff that rivals in size the entire university's advancement office of just a few decades ago.

Of course, as discussed earlier, most people do not join a council only to give and raise money, and most presidents and deans do not view their councils only in fundraising terms. However, unless a discussion of fundraising is a part of council meetings at least occasionally, the council may come to view it as something the president or the advancement staff does. They may applaud the results but may not be inspired to add their own participation.

It is relatively safe to discuss corporate or foundation prospects or opportunities for government support, and council members may be able to help open doors, build relationships, or even serve as advocates for the institution within those organizations. Discussing individual donor prospects in such settings, however, is a more sensitive matter. If the council is more than several people, some likely will feel inhibited from providing information about others or even hearing about the institution's plans for soliciting prospects. The larger the group, the less productive such discussions are likely to be.

Inviting the advisory council to identify goals and objectives for a campaign can be especially useful. Their perceptions may reflect those of the institution's broader constituency, and the council may serve as a focus group to help determine items that have the greatest attraction to donors. It also may encourage them to think about their own role in the campaign in terms of leadership and support.

Some people say that presenting a summary of the council's own giving at every meeting is important. That may be an appropriate agenda item for a council that has a giving expectation of its members or that includes fundraising among its stated purposes, but in reality, presidents and deans should use good judgment about when and how to discuss the

45

council's giving. For example, if some council members are giving generously while others are not, calling attention to the deficiencies could negatively affect those who are doing their share. If giving is expected and some council members are not participating, the problem must be addressed in a way that does not adversely affect the morale of the overall council. It may be best to address problem situations privately with the nonparticipants.

Of course, if the council is performing well in giving and fundraising, that should be cause for congratulations from the chair and expressions of gratitude from the president or dean. It can be very useful for the chair and the president or dean to acknowledge particularly generous council members in front of their peers during the meeting. It is a rare individual who does not appreciate that type of recognition, and providing it helps raise the sights of others who hear it. Ultimately, it is better for discussions in council meetings to be positive. Concerns about any members who are not meeting expectations should be expressed to them privately, perhaps by the council chair, a development committee chair, or campaign chair as seems appropriate.

SOCIAL EVENTS. Social activities and networking opportunities are important components of any group's activities. As discussed earlier, the social and potential business contacts are often motivations for serving on an advisory council. There is also the pure enjoyment of the camaraderie that comes from working with others on a shared task.

The type of social activity included in advisory council meetings varies depending on the membership, its geographic distribution, the location of the campus, and other considerations. Some meetings may be confined to a single day, perhaps with a break for lunch or dinner or both. Others begin with a dinner the night before the meeting, perhaps including spouses, with the formal work beginning the next morning. Meetings also can coincide with other campus activities, such as athletic events or artistic performances that incorporate social time into the council's overall experience.

Interacting with Students and Faculty

MANY PRESIDENTS AND DEANS value opportunities for the advisory council to interact with faculty and students. One (perhaps courageous) dean described a tradition at her institution:

> Our council has unstructured panel discussions with students with all university employees OUT of the room. Council members say this is easily the most enlightening—and fun—part of the entire meeting. Students are selected by major, gender, class year, ethnicity, and other characteristics. It is a usually a panel of between four and six students, which meets with the council for an hour.

There is, of course, the risk that the council will take up faculty or student issues and exacerbate pressures on the president or the dean. Nevertheless, faculty and students are the essence of the institution, and many council members will want to hear their views. In addition, they are usually positive and pleasant company. It is better to initiate opportunities for the council to interact with students and faculty than to leave it to chance. I once knew a trustee who would arrive in town the afternoon before the scheduled meeting to take a long walk around the campus, randomly stopping students and asking about their experience at the institution. He would report his findings at the board meeting, sometimes creating a diversion from the scheduled agenda to pursue an unrepresentative problem mentioned by a single student. Arranging structured settings for board members to talk with a representative group of students and/or faculty seems a better way to provide such communication.

Some presidents and deans offered examples of how students are involved in their advisory council meetings:

- We schedule presentations at the council meeting by students about class projects and internship experiences.

- Council meetings include presentations by student teams that have participated in national competitions.

- We invite selected students to all council dinners and social events.

47

Having opportunities to talk with professors and students is part of the "something different" that many council members view as a benefit of their service. Most will be business professionals who find it interesting and stimulating to engage with individuals whose perspectives are different from those of their usual associates.

Bringing Boards and Councils Together

IF ADVISORY BOARDS AND COUNCILS are to serve as sources of future leadership for the institution—that is, places to try out individuals who may eventually join a governing or foundation board—then it is important for members of those other boards to become acquainted with council members. It is also advantageous for individuals who serve one college or school to have opportunities to gain a wider perspective and become familiar with other units and programs of the university. The broader exposure can be interesting and enriching. It also helps increase the networking value of council membership and signals to members that they are a valued component of the institution's leadership.

Some institutional advisory councils attend joint events with the governing board; for example, some councils meet around the same time as the board of trustees, allowing for a social event or dinner with both groups. Athletic events, performances, and other major events are also opportunities to bring advisory council members together with others. The George Washington University Leadership Retreat offers an example of a special initiative to bring the volunteer leadership of a university together in the context of preparing for a campaign. (See Appendix II.)

Communication and Involvement between Meetings

PRESIDENTS AND DEANS IN THE SURVEY emphasized the need to commit time to build relationships with advisory council members and maintain communication between meetings. Some do so by sending regular e-mails, newsletters, and copies of other campus publications. Some meet with small groups of advisory council members between meetings or visit with them during outreach events in their home cities. Others make efforts to involve council members in the life of the institution by recruiting them as guest speakers, career advisors, or other roles. One dean explained how council members assist in student recruitment: "We have [council members] who open their homes to host high school students or bring the best grads from their local high schools to campus. [They] can help us in connecting with the best prospects." Another dean explained, "We try to find ways to involve the board members outside of the regular meetings, for example, participating on a program review committee, serving as the board representative to the alumni association, or helping to implement a key technology initiative."

Some highlighted the importance of providing feedback to the council regarding their recommendations, even if that feedback is to explain why they could not be implemented. As one dean wrote, "These are busy people. They don't want to waste their time. They want to know that their advice has been taken seriously and at least considered, or they will stop participating in meetings."

Formal meetings of the advisory board or council are just one aspect of cultivating a relationship between the members and the institution. As discussed earlier, involvement is the key to building a relationship that will turn outsiders into insiders, help them identify with the needs and aspirations of the institution, and lead to support—both financially and in other forms. Universities, colleges, and schools can maximize the value of their councils through multifaceted and continuous efforts to build these relationships throughout the year.

Questions for Presidents, Chancellors, and Deans

- Have you assigned sufficient staff to manage the advisory council, ensure its meetings are well-planned, and maintain communication between meetings?

- Have you committed enough of your own time to cultivate relationships with members of the advisory council?

- Do your council meetings reflect an appropriate balance of presentations, discussion of issues, and social activities?

- Have you addressed the council's role in giving and fundraising? If fundraising is a part of its mission, is the topic discussed at most meetings and in an appropriate manner?

- Do you involve students and faculty in council meetings or activities in a useful and appropriate way?

- Do you provide feedback to the council on any actions taken, or not taken, as a result of their recommendations?

- Do you maintain contact with the council between meetings and try to involve them in the life of the university, college, or school?

CHAPTER 5

The Bottom Line: Costs and Benefits

THE 2006 AGB SURVEY WAS THE FIRST to collect comprehensive data on advisory boards and councils in higher education, both those related to an entire institution and those that serve an individual college or school within a university. Hundreds of presidents and deans responded with a wealth of ideas, examples, opinions, and advice.

So, what's the bottom line? Are advisory boards and councils worth the effort and expense? Do they make positive contributions to their institutions, enable presidents and deans to do a better job, help their institutions advance, strengthen relationships outside the campus, provide a cadre of donors and future institutional leaders, and provide other benefits so often associated with boards? Most presidents and deans said yes.

The survey asked them to evaluate the overall value of their councils by selecting a statement that "most closely agrees with your assessment of the contribution of your advisory board or council to your institution." Seventy-eight percent of presidents and 81 percent of deans selected "it is helpful to the university, college, or school." Another 17 percent of presidents and 15 percent of deans said the council is potentially helpful to their institutions, but acknowledged that theirs is not currently working as it should. Only 5 percent of presidents and 4 percent of deans provided negative answers. A few comments suggested a situation in which an advisory council caused problems. On the whole, and in overwhelming percentages, presidents and deans find their advisory boards and councils helpful to them personally and of benefit to their institution, college, or school.

That said, they do involve some costs and risks. The costs are not just budgetary; they also include a commitment of the president's or dean's time, which may be among the dearest of commodities. Principal risks include the possibility of the council going beyond its mission of advising and beginning to think or behave like a governing board, attempting to influence decisions outside its scope of responsibility. A related risk is that the council becomes just another constituency, making demands on the president or dean or taking up the issues of other campus groups. A third, somewhat opposite risk—is that the council becomes a laidback social club, requiring resources of time and money to sustain but contributing little wealth or wisdom to the institution.

In other words, advisory councils can make important contributions—both financial and otherwise—but they must be managed well in order to avoid the pitfalls and realize their full value to the institution. Like anything else in life, success requires work.

Advisory Council Best Practices

APPENDIX III OF THIS BOOK includes selected quotes from survey participants and captures the flavor as well as the substance of their thoughts. Although there clearly were different opinions on various issues, there were some consistent themes among presidents and deans, both in response to AGB's online survey and in my personal conversations with them.

The idea of best practices is, of course, complicated. It is relatively easy to identify practices that are universally bad, but what may be best in one setting may not be effective in another, so it is difficult to identify a universal best. Colleges and universities are different from each other in their histories, cultures, locations, and the programs they offer, among other variables. Presidents and deans have different backgrounds, experiences, and skills. They have different needs and expectations for their advisory boards and councils. The council must be designed and managed in a manner consistent with the unique circumstances.

The following are some recommended practices for the organization and management of advisory boards and councils. Some reflect consensus among the presidents and deans who participated in the survey, while others are my opinion, based both on the AGB study and my professional experience. The following points may not be provable best practices, but they at least define areas for presidents, chancellors, and deans to consider carefully when establishing or working with advisory boards and councils.

DEFINE A CLEAR PURPOSE FOR THE ADVISORY BOARD OR COUNCIL. Many study participants—regardless of their council's purpose—emphasized the importance of the president, chancellor, or dean knowing exactly what he or she wants from the advisory council and council members. Some presidents and deans see their advisory councils primarily as vehicles for engaging and cultivating new donors. Others see them as providing valuable connections to a community, government, or some other important constituency. Some deans value them as a source of leverage within the university—in other words, a group of credible outsiders who add weight to the dean's vision and plans for the college or school. Some value their councils most for their candid advice and fresh perspective. All are valid reasons for starting or maintaining an advisory council.

Some respondents prefer to keep the purposes of the council flexible, but in my opinion, the purposes should be articulated clearly in writing and communicated to members of the council, both as they are enlisted and periodically during their service. Without clear purposes the council may become an uninspiring experience for its members with little or no benefit to the institution. At worst, the council may wander into areas beyond its purview and become a source of tension and political risk.

ESTABLISH AND COMMUNICATE A CLEAR STRUCTURE. Not every president or dean agrees with the need for formal advisory council bylaws or guidelines. Some prefer to keep their advisory councils informal and flexible, a kind of kitchen cabinet that advises the president or dean on call. That is, of course, quite acceptable if it serves the purposes the president or dean has in mind and if it is permitted under the institution's policies. However, such informality has downsides, too.

First, total informality does not convey the advisory council's importance to its members. Without standards or rules individuals may have difficulty seeing service as worthy of commitment. In addition, having no written guidelines on membership, terms of service, attendance, and other matters leaves the dean or president no option for ridding the council of an unproductive, or even disruptive, member without such action becoming personal. The president or dean also may find difficult turning down anyone who expresses interest, eventually filling the council with people of uneven, and possibly mediocre, quality. Such a scenario could lower the overall standing of the council and the tone of its discussions.

Unless the institution's policies require them, advisory councils do not need formal bylaws. However, I have found that having at least some clear statement of mission, criteria for membership, and policies about size, meeting frequency, member expectations, and terms of service is important to avoid misunderstandings and awkward situations and to keep the council properly focused on its mission. These policies may be communicated in a brief, succinct document—perhaps no more than a page or two—and both current and prospective council members should receive and understand them.

On matters of council organization and operation, each council should be designed to meet the particular needs of each institution. It may be advisable to consider the normative ranges and practices reported in the survey:

51

- About 20 to 30 members

- Fixed, two to three year terms, renewable up to two or three times

- Appointment by the president or dean (or both) from candidates suggested by current council members, the advancement office, and other sources

- Meetings two to four times per year; agenda sent in advance of meetings; minutes taken and distributed following meetings

- Required attendance at a minimum of one to two meetings per year

- A chair or cochairs, either appointed by the president/dean or elected by the council, serving a fixed term

- Committees or task forces created only to serve identifiable, specific purposes

SELECT MEMBERS TO SERVE THE PURPOSES. If the primary purpose of an advisory council is to raise funds, then appointing members from diverse backgrounds may not be important. Likewise, if the council's purpose is to improve relationships with neighbors and the local government, a membership of corporate chief executives may not be the best choice. As architects say, "Form follows function." The council's purposes must come first; then membership can be designed to support them.

Some presidents and deans advised that it is best to start with people who are already familiar with and have some commitment to the institution, perhaps alumni or well-known business leaders. Others advised that when adding new members, it is important to make sure they are thoroughly vetted and to seek input from existing council members before proceeding with the appointment.

Recognizing that councils serve various purposes and should fit the needs of the particular institution, and acknowledging that some prefer larger councils, I generally favor being selective and keeping standards high. Individuals of influence, affluence, and prestige prefer to serve on boards with peers. That does not mean that every member of the council should be a chief executive officer or billionaire. Business professionals enjoy interacting with distinguished academics, medical experts, political officials, nonprofit executives, and leaders in other fields. They likely will enjoy hearing from those who have varied experiences. However, people who are distinguished may not enjoy discussions with others less accomplished. One of the problems with a council that is too large is that it may not be possible to maintain consistent standards.

As some presidents and deans pointed out, it can be very difficult to change the purpose of an existing council. Members selected with one purpose in mind are not easily moved aside if the president or dean determines the council should serve a different purpose than originally intended. This again suggests the value of clarifying the council's purpose at the outset and selecting members consistent with that vision. If there is a need to change the purposes of an existing council, a practical strategy may be to create an additional group rather than encouraging the existing group to undertake new roles to which they never agreed and for which they may in fact be ill-equipped.

52

INVOLVE THE COUNCIL IN SUBSTANCE AND ASSIGN SPECIFIC WORK. The need to avoid a constant diet of "show and tell" was among the most frequent recommendations offered by presidents and deans, and I strongly endorse the point. People join advisory councils for social and business contacts, for the prestige, and for the experience as well as the desire to serve. Motivations are often mixed, but none are likely to enjoy or continue serving as an audience for hours of presentations about the glories of the institution and its leaders. Identify real issues and important questions for the council to consider and allow time for open and forthright discussion.

Of course, presidents and deans must use judgment when selecting subjects for the council's consideration. There is no need to air dirty laundry, and it would be inappropriate to discuss such sensitive matters as personnel performance. It also may be unwise to ask the council's advice on matters over which the president or dean has no control or that are clearly the purview of another authority, such as the institution's governing board or faculty. Nevertheless, the opportunity to deepen the council members' commitment to the institution's goals is likely to offset the risks from engaging them in open dialogue on real issues with the institution's other important constituencies—including faculty and students.

Take time to plan council meetings and the specific work the council is to perform. Clearly defining the council's tasks will enhance the odds that its members will find satisfaction in having achieved something concrete. Inviting the council to a discussion without focus may become a rambling conversation that leads in unanticipated directions.

HAVE CLEAR EXPECTATIONS FOR GIVING AND FUNDRAISING. I believe advisory councils should have an expectation for giving by its members, at least at a level commensurate with each member's capacity. Whether to establish a minimum annual gift is a separate question with arguments on both sides, as discussed in Chapter 2. If individuals who are so closely and deeply involved in the life of the college or university do not support it at any level, others may question why they should. The more prestigious and visible the advisory council, the more important the example of its members is in influencing the behavior of others.

Still, not all presidents and deans agree with my view on this subject. Some say fundraising is the primary purpose of their councils; others say it is one of several purposes; a few say that fundraising should not be a part of the council's purpose at all. Regardless, most agree that if fundraising is at all a purpose of the council, or if giving is an expectation of council members, then those expectations and requirements should be clear. They should be communicated explicitly, both in the process of enlisting council members and as a part of its meeting agendas.

If giving at some level is a requirement of council membership, it should be enforced except under unusual circumstances. Otherwise, it may undermine the morale of those who do meet their obligations. It may be best for the council chair, or perhaps an advancement committee chair, to undertake a conversation with members who do not meet giving expectations, so as not to compromise the relationship between the president or dean and the recalcitrant member. Individuals who accept the chair position on a council with such a requirement should understand that ensuring expected participation by council members is one of their responsibilities. If members do not participate as expected, their terms should not be renewed.

BUILD RELATIONSHIPS AND ENGAGE THE COUNCIL MEMBERS BETWEEN MEETINGS. Relationships cannot develop from spending a few hours a year together. As many presidents and deans advised, it is important to communicate with council members between meetings and involve them as much as possible in the ongoing life of the institution. Invite them to participate in social and academic activities—to counsel students, to present guest lectures, to attend football games, or whatever other opportunities arise. Convening the council just twice a year and ignoring its members the rest of the time will not make it a group of individuals committed to its purposes; presidents and deans must do more to gain the council's commitment or to build its members' identification with the institution. It is advisable for the president or dean to collaborate with the advancement office in working with advisory council members, because advancement systems include methods of tracking contacts and relationship status and can provide regular reminders to initiate communications.

CONSIDER THE COUNCIL'S ADVICE AND PROVIDE FEEDBACK. If the council offers advice, the president or dean should consider it and provide feedback to the council on what, if any, action has been taken. I agree with study participants who commented that it is not advisable to reject the council's recommendations outright, especially in the context of a meeting. It is acceptable, however, to check them out, discuss them with others, and then inform the council with good reasons the advice cannot be implemented. Even better, if their recommendations can be adopted, in whole or in part, their impact on the university, college, or school should be shared in concrete terms.

Look for opportunities to illustrate and dramatize the council's contributions. Take the council on tours of buildings they helped build, laboratories they helped equip, and so forth. Have faculty or students speak to the council about changes in their work that the council helped initiate.

COMMIT SUFFICIENT BUDGET AND STAFF SUPPORT. Managing an advisory council well requires time and effort. The president or dean simply will not have the time to provide personally all of the support and communication required. A person on the president's or dean's staff or someone in the advancement office may support the council as a board secretary. Responses to the AGB study reflect varied practices on this point.

Based on my experience, if the advancement office manages the council program and its activities, some cautions are in order. First, make sure that staff who manage the council do not view it exclusively as a volunteer fundraising committee, even if fundraising is one of its primary purposes. At the same time, make sure their performance objectives properly reflect their overall portfolio, as managing the advisory council does not always relate to fundraising. In other words, if fundraisers are expected to complete a certain number of solicitations or meet specific fundraising targets, their work with the council may detract from the time available for such activities, and that reality should be reflected in their performance review.

Recognize, too, that there is an opportunity cost when fundraisers assume increased administrative duties, as it reduces their face time with donors and prospects. There is a hazard, particularly for advancement staff based in a college's or school's advancement office. They may be accountable for fundraising performance to a central advancement office while also addressing the dean's need for staff support on non-fundraising matters, like an advisory council. Individuals in that position can feel caught between conflicting goals and expectations. It may be more effective to assign the day-to-day management of council activities to someone other than a major gift officer, and keep the major gift officer engaged with individual council members and the process of building the dean's relationship with those who are prospects for significant support.

ENCOURAGE AND SUPPORT THE INVOLVEMENT OF ADVISORY COUNCIL MEMBERS IN OTHER AREAS OF THE OVERALL INSTITUTION. Many individuals will seek a broader involvement with the institution than service to a single college or school. They may wish to serve eventually on the governing or foundation board; they may seek to build relationships with volunteer leaders of other parts of the institution; or they may want to learn about the programs and activities of the broader university. If they serve on a president's advisory council, they may also wish to deepen their knowledge of the programs of one of the university's schools. Many individuals want to be involved in various ways. They may have many interests and belong to more than one group serving an institution. In my experience, their service to the part and to the whole is often enhanced by their exposure and engagement at multiple levels.

TAKE THE COUNCIL SERIOUSLY. Advisory boards and councils do not have governing authority. The president or dean does not work for them. However, as one respondent advised, "Treat them as if they are members of your board of trustees." Prepare for their meetings, take their advice seriously, respond to their communications, share with them the true realities of the challenges you face as a president or dean, and be proactive in building relationships with council members. Bring them inside and make them owners of your institution. To do otherwise is to disrespect the commitment they have made, to waste their time, and to forgo the opportunities that their involvement and support can provide—to the institution itself and to the president or dean with whom they serve.

Advice to Members of Advisory Boards and Councils

ALTHOUGH THIS BOOK has been directed primarily at presidents and deans—who often initiate, appoint, and essentially lead the advisory boards and councils that serve their institutions—and at the advancement officers and other staff who support the councils' work, it concludes with some recommendations to the council members themselves. Because the AGB study did not seek responses from members of advisory boards or councils, the following recommendations do not represent a consensus of their views. Rather, they are my recommendations, which are generally mirror images of the suggestions offered to presidents and deans.

BE CLEAR ABOUT THE PURPOSE OF THE ADVISORY BOARD OR COUNCIL BEFORE ACCEPTING MEMBERSHIP. Is the purpose of the board or council primarily to provide advice, to serve as the institution's advocates and ambassadors, to give and raise funds, or some combination? Are the purposes defined in some document, such as bylaws or guidelines? Can the president or dean offer some examples of how the council has made a difference for the institution in the past? If not, you may question why serving on the council will be a good use of your time and energy.

CAREFULLY CONSIDER YOUR OWN MOTIVATIONS FOR SERVING ON THE BOARD OR COUNCIL. There is nothing sinister about serving on a board or council in part because it provides the potential of new social or business contacts or because it provides a pleasant and interesting relief from the daily routines of your professional life. However, the institution has needs that it is hoping you will help meet, whether they are for financial resources, expertise, or relationships in the broader community. Before joining, be sure that you can and are willing to sacrifice the time and effort to be an active participant and engage your own networks of friends and associates on behalf of the college or university as it may expect.

CONSIDER THE OTHER MEMBERS OF THE BOARD OR COUNCIL AND THINK ABOUT WHAT YOU ADD. Review the names and backgrounds of others who serve on the advisory board or council. How does you experience and expertise fit in? Will you be able to add something new to the discussion or do your skills just replicate those already present? Is this a group with which you will feel comfortable working? If the answers to those questions are not evident, then it may not be the right assignment.

BE PREPARED TO MAKE AN APPROPRIATE FINANCIAL COMMITMENT. Whether the board or council requires giving by its members or not, your position as a member of the institution's leadership group makes your giving—or lack thereof—visible to others. Personal support from members of the institution's family—including the governing board, advisory council, foundation board, and alumni association board—makes a statement about their commitment to the institution and the worthiness of its cause. Without such a demonstration of support from those who know the institution best, appeals to others less directly involved may carry less credibility. To be surprised in this regard could be embarrassing and disappointing, so make sure you understand what level of commitment is expected.

REMEMBER YOUR APPROPRIATE ROLE. An advisory board or council is not the governing board of the institution and does not have legal authority or responsibility for its programs, assets, or personnel. In general, as the survey results suggest, most advisory boards and councils belong to the presidents and deans who create, appoint, support, and sustain them. As a member of such a board, you can contribute by responding to the president's or dean's assignments and challenges as best you can and heeding your advisory role by refraining from deliberations that are within the purview of the faculty, governing board, or some other body. To do otherwise is likely to cause embarrassment, mar your reputation, and damage the institution.

INSIST ON DISCUSSIONS OF REAL QUESTIONS AND ISSUES, NOT JUST MEETINGS OF SHOW-AND-TELL BY THE INSTITUTION'S LEADERS AND FACULTY. If you have been invited to serve on an advisory board or council, you are probably a successful and respected professional. You are busy, and you can find many opportunities to listen to speeches. If the council meetings consist entirely of presentations about the institution's programs and achievements, it is unlikely to be interesting or productive. If you end up in such a situation, just explain to the president or dean that your schedule is tight and that you do not wish to be reappointed when your current term expires.

EXPECT YOUR ADVICE TO BE TAKEN SERIOUSLY AND INSIST ON FEEDBACK ON WHAT ACTIONS, IF ANY, WERE TAKEN AS A RESULT. If the president or dean asks for your advice but then does not go the additional step of considering it—perhaps by conferring with the faculty, more senior levels of the administration, the governing board, or others as may be appropriate—you have reason to question whether your time on the council is well spent and what the real purposes of its existence may be. Colleges and universities are complex. The various political, financial, or other considerations may make it difficult or impossible to implement the advice of individuals external to the institution, regardless of their experience or professional achievement. Be prepared to accept that reality. Of course, if the council's advice always proves impossible to implement and consistently seems to have no impact, then you are right to question its continued value and purpose.

56

GET TO KNOW THE INSTITUTION AND ITS PEOPLE. Invest the time to become acquainted with the president or dean, faculty members, and students. As part of an organized effort, it is valuable for the advisory council to visit classes, meet with students, tour campus buildings, and hear from faculty about their research and writing. You will find your service on the board or council more interesting and rewarding, and you will be a more effective advocate for the institution if you are able to speak knowledgeably about its people and programs.

TAKE PRIDE AND SATISFACTION FROM YOUR WORK. As the presidents and deans who responded to AGB's survey made clear, their advisory boards and councils are important to them and to their institutions. Your participation as a member of such a group represents a significant sacrifice of your time and effort and a sharing of your intellectual and emotional energy. Whatever benefits you may derive as an individual from the activity, your voluntary service on a board or council is an enormous resource that advances higher education, strengthens colleges and universities, and enriches the lives of students.

Conclusion

GOVERNING BOARDS CAN NO LONGER DO IT ALONE. They face increasing, and sometimes competing, pressures to govern better while also increasing their effectiveness as advocates and fundraisers. They are expected to bring specialized skills and experiences to the board table, while also giving more and participating in fundraising to secure their institutions' futures.

Not only president and chancellors, but also deans and program directors are now significantly involved in planning, fundraising, and building external relationships for their colleges, schools, and programs. Faced with such responsibilities, they need the advice and support of volunteer leaders; not all such needs can be met by the governing board alone. In this environment, advisory boards and councils have come to play a vital role in the leadership of colleges and universities and in the advancement of higher education.

I hope this book will prove useful to both campus officers and the individuals who serve on advisory councils, to increase their awareness of their important contributions to their institutions and to make council service a more rewarding and enjoyable experience.

Sample Advisory Council Bylaws and Guidelines

EXAMPLE #1

BYLAWS OF THE COLLEGE OF LIBERAL ARTS AND SCIENCES DEAN'S ADVISORY COUNCIL IOWA STATE UNIVERSITY AMES, IOWA

I. Purpose

The College of Liberal Arts and Sciences Dean's Advisory Council is a group of business, government, academic, and professional leaders who are interested in the vitality of the College of Liberal Arts and Sciences at Iowa State University. The council advises the College of Liberal Arts and Sciences to strengthen its learning, research, and outreach programs, improve its facilities, expand its base of support, and serve its alumni.

II. Membership

The College of Liberal Arts and Sciences Dean's Advisory Council is composed of a maximum of 30 members.

The members are appointed by Iowa State University's dean of liberal arts and sciences with advice from current council members and LAS academic department chairs. The term of membership is three years with a maximum of two consecutive terms. Terms will be staggered so that ten members will be appointed or reappointed each year. Retiring members are eligible for reappointment after a one-year period. The membership year begins at adjournment of the spring meeting of the council and extends to adjournment of the next spring meeting.

Members that replace resigning Council members will serve out that member's remaining term. Terms of two years or more constitute a full-term membership and members are eligible to serve one additional term. Members serving less than two years of a term are eligible to serve two additional terms.

Vacant terms will be appointed by the dean of liberal arts and sciences with advice from the Council chair.

Membership of the council is expected to be representative of the diverse activities and constituencies of the college and may include Iowa State alumni, retired faculty and staff, and friends.

The dean and associate deans of the College of Liberal Arts and Sciences are ex-officio members of the council. The Office of the Dean acts as secretariat for the council.

III. Officers

The officers of the council consist of the chair, chair-elect, and past chair; they are elected from the membership of the council. The term of service of the officers is one year. They are eligible for re-election for one additional term. The officers are chosen without regard for their normal period of service on the council, and their appointment is automatically extended until the end of their tenure in office if their three-year term as member expires during their term of service.

The chair shall preside over meetings of the council and provide guidance in achievement of its goals. The chair-elect shall preside over council meetings in the absence of the chair and has responsibility for coordinating the activities of the ad hoc committees of the council with the exception of the nominating committee. The past-chair serves as chair of the nominating committee. Members of the nominating committee are appointed annually by the chair of the council.

Election of the chair-elect takes place at the spring meeting of the council. A simple majority of votes cast by members present is required for election.

IV. Meetings

The council normally meets in the spring and in the fall of each academic year. In addition to the two regular meetings held each year, special meetings of the council and of its committees may be called by the chair. The council normally acts as a committee of the whole, but committees may be appointed by the chair to undertake specific assignments.

The chair, in collaboration with the dean, sets the dates for meetings of the council. The Office of the Dean is responsible for arrangements and, in collaboration with the chair, prepares the agendum for each meeting and mails it to all members of the council at least ten days prior to each meeting. At the end of each meeting, the council makes suggestions for the agendum for the next meeting.

V. Bylaws Revision

Revisions to the bylaws can be proposed by any council member and by Iowa State University's Dean of the College of Liberal Arts and Sciences. Proposed revisions must be distributed in writing to all members of the council at least ten days prior to the meeting where action on the proposals will be taken. A two-thirds majority of votes cast by all members present and absentee votes is required for approval.

VI. Disclaimer of Liability

The council does, by this article, for itself and on behalf of its individual members, disclaim any and all liability for any losses, claims, demands, or actions arising or resulting from the recommendations or advice made or given in good faith to Iowa State University pursuant to the activities anticipated herein. It is intended that Iowa State University exercise independent judgment and evaluate for itself the usefulness of the advice and recommendations so given.

Source: Iowa State University College of Arts and Sciences, *http://www.las.iastate.edu/alumni/bylaws.shtml* (accessed February 4, 2007).

58

EXAMPLE #2

MODEL BYLAWS OF THE UNIVERSITY OF TEXAS (INSTITUTION) (SCHOOL OR UNIT) ADVISORY COUNCIL

Article I Authorization

Section 1. This advisory council is established pursuant to the *Rules and Regulations* of the Board of Regents of the University of Texas System (Regents' *Rules*) and shall be called the University of Texas (*institution*) (*school or unit*) Advisory Council (Council).[1]

Section 2. The University of Texas (*institution*) (*school or unit*) Advisory Council is part of the University of Texas (*institution*). In accordance with the Regents' *Rules*, the Advisory Council is responsible to the (dean or director) of (school or unit) and the president of the University of Texas (*institution*).[2] All activities of the University of Texas (*institution*) (*school or unit*) Advisory Council shall be subject to the Regents' *Rules*; the rules and policies of the University of Texas (*institution*) and the University of Texas System.

Article II Responsibilities and Duties

Section 1. The University of Texas (*institution*) (the school, college or other comparable teaching or research unit) Advisory Council is an advisory organization and shall serve the (*school or unit*) in a manner determined by the dean or director of the unit subject to the approval of the institution's president.[3] The (*school or unit*) Advisory Council shall work with the (*dean or director*), the president and the (*institution's chief development officer or equivalent*) to determine its role in seeking private support.[4]

Article III Membership

Section 1. *Membership.* The University of Texas (*institution*) (*school or unit*) Advisory Council shall consist of (*number*) members recommended by the (*dean or director*) of the (*school or unit*) and appointed by the president of the University of Texas (*institution*) (*school or unit*).[5] The president shall, in consultation with the (*dean or director*) of (*school or unit*), adopt guidelines for the appointment and/or reappointment of members of the Advisory Council that are consistent with the Regents' *Rules*.[6] The president shall ensure that at the time of their

---

1   Presently under Series 60302, creation of an advisory council requires approval from the institution's president, the appropriate Executive Vice Chancellor, the Chancellor and the Board of Regents. The proposed amended version adds the Vice Chancellor for External Relations as an additional person from whom approval must be obtained. Consideration should be given to amending this Rule further so that the president of the institution is delegated this authority.

2   Regents' *Rules*, Series 60302, Sections 1 and 4.

3   Regents' *Rules*, Series, 60302, Section 2.

4   Regents' *Rules*, Series 60302, Section 1.

5   Currently the Regents *Rules*, the Board of Regents' has delegated "final approval" of membership to the Chancellor following consultation with the appropriate Executive Vice Chancellor. Consideration should to be given to allowing membership to be finalized at the institutional level. (See proposed amended *Rules*, Series 60302, Section 3).

6   Series 60302, Section 3 requires membership guidelines to give consideration to "appropriate balance in advisory council membership, including concerns relating to gender, ethnicity, years of involvement or experience with the college, school or unit, geographical distribution, and the special needs of the school, college, or unit."

appointment, each individual member receives a copy of these Bylaws and is notified of their term of office along with the expectations and responsibilities of membership. The membership roster of the Council shall be reported to the Vice Chancellor for External Relations by (*date prior to September 1st*), or as otherwise designated, of each year. The president and the (*dean or director*) of (school or unit) shall be ex-officio members with voting privileges.[7] *(Each advisory council should limit the number of voting members. However, if practical, each advisory council may have several other categories of membership that do not have voting privileges. These additional categories of membership must be structured so as to benefit the advisory council and may be designed so as to recognize valuable service to an advisory council or to express high esteem for particular past or present members.)*

Section 2. *Term of Appointment.* All members shall serve for (*one or other reasonable number*) (*three or other reasonable time period*)-year term with the option to be re-appointed for (*one or other reasonable number*) additional (*three or other reasonable time period*)-year term. Terms of appointment are staggered so that only a (*one-third or other reasonable portion*) of the membership terms expire each year. Each term begins on September 1 of the appointment year.[8] The president has discretion to relieve any member of the Advisory Council from membership prior to the end of the member's term of appointment.

Section 3. *Duty of Members and Conflict of Interest.*[9] It shall be the duty of each member to conduct any efforts undertaken on behalf of the Council within the scope of the responsibilities and duties of the Council as provided in the Bylaws and in compliance with the Regents' *Rules* and University policy. It shall be the duty of each individual member to avoid conflicts of interest.

A "conflict of interest" exists when a member has a personal or private relationship or interest that could reasonably be expected to diminish the member's independence of judgment in performing official duties. Examples include a member's financial interest in an entity that is transacting business with the University of Texas (institution), the University of Texas (institution) (school or unit) Advisory Council, or the U.T. System; or the member's solicitation or acceptance of a gift, favor, service, or other benefit that might reasonably tend to influence the member in performing official duties, or that a member knows or should know is being offered with that intent.

A member who becomes aware of a conflict of interest must provide timely written notice to the Council chair and the president. The president shall take appropriate steps to address any conflicts of interest of which he or she is made aware.

60

---

7   Regents' *Rules*, Series 60302, Section 5. In the proposed amended version of Series 60301, Section 5, *Reporting and Budget*, accurate rosters are to be forwarded to the Chancellor via the Vice Chancellor for External Relations annually. As currently written, Series 60301 states that "accurate rosters" of a development board's membership are to be forwarded to the Chancellor via the Vice Chancellor for External Relations "annually" while Series 60302, *Advisory Councils of an Institution*, states that the accurate rosters of advisory council members are to be forwarded by July 15th of each year. The best approach would be to make the date for submitting accurate rosters the same for both entities. In the draft of the proposed bylaws for both Development Boards and for Advisory Councils, both organizations can choose a date for the annual roster report that is prior to September 1st.

8   Regents' *Rules*, Series 60302, Section 3.

9   Regents' *Rules*, Series 30104. See also "Ethics and The University of Texas System—A Brief Practical Guide" *http://www.utsystem.edu/ogc/Ethics/Ethguide.htm.*

Article IV Officers

Section 1. *Manner of Election.* The election of new officers and new Council membership rules and policies shall proceed by voice vote.

Section 2. *Number of Officers.* The officers of the Council shall be a chair, chair-elect, and a vice-chair, who shall be members of the Council. *(Each Advisory Council may have additional officers as is necessary to conduct the duties of the Council.)*

Section 3. *Election of Officers and Term of Office.* Each officer of the Council shall be elected by a majority of the voting members of the Council and shall hold office for _____ year(s).

Section 4. *Schedule of Elections.* Officers shall be elected _____ (*insert timeframe—annually or other reasonable time period*) at the regular (*fall, spring, or other*) meeting of the Board.

Section 5. *Duties of Chair.* The chair shall preside at all meetings of the Council; shall be responsible for the general direction of the affairs of the Council, and shall be the official representative of the Council. The chair shall ensure that an accurate copy of the Bylaws are filed with (*dean or director*), president, (*the institution's chief development officer or similar administrator*) and the Vice Chancellor for External Relations. The chair shall cause accurate minutes of the Council's proceedings to be kept, and shall file copies of all minutes with the (*dean or director*), president, (institution's chief development officer or similar administrator). The chair shall, in conjunction with (*institution's chief development officer or similar administrator*), be responsible for complying with any reporting requirements regarding plans, programs and activities of the Advisory Council.

In addition to his or her duty to disclose Conflicts of Interest as required by Article III, Section 3, the chair shall review all such disclosures, cooperate as directed with the actions of the president in response to such disclosures, (*and as appropriate, report the disclosure and related action to the relevant Advisory Council Committee*). The chair shall likewise report to the (*dean or director*) and the president any material problems identified by Advisory Council members. In the absence or disability of the chair, the chair-elect shall preside and serve in his place.

Article V Finances

Financial support of the University of Texas (*school or unit*) Advisory Council shall be provided exclusively by the budget of the University of Texas (*school or unit*). Such budgets will be made through established budgetary procedures.[10] The Advisory Council's receipts and expenses must be budgeted and accounted for in separate accounts. The accounts must be specifically identifiable in the detail of the operating budget.[11]

Article VI Meetings

Section 1. The University of Texas (*institution*) (*school or unit*) Advisory Council shall hold at least (*two or other reasonable number that is more than one*) regular meetings each year, (*one or more*) in the (*fall, spring, or other*) and (*one or more*) in the (*fall, spring, or other*); the (*fall, spring, or other*) meeting shall be considered the annual meeting.

---

10 Regents' *Rules*, Series 60302, Section 5.

11 Regents' *Rules*, Series 60302, Section 5. Source: Associate Vice Chancellor-Controller and Chief Budget Officer's April 14, 2004 directive to the institutions.

Section 2. Special meetings of the Council shall be held as determined by the Council or upon call of the chair or upon request in writing signed by at least three members. There shall be at least three days' prior written notice of such special meetings to all members of the Advisory Council. The president or (*dean or director*) may call meetings as he or she deems necessary.

Section 3. The exact date and place of holding meetings shall be as fixed by the Council, or in the call issued for the meeting.

Section 4. Decisions will be made by a majority vote of those members present in person at the meeting.

Article VII Quorum

_____ voting members shall constitute a quorum.

Article VIII Committees

The chair is authorized to establish such committees as he or she may deem appropriate.

Article IX Internal Foundations

Pursuant to the Regents' *Rules*, any internal foundation that has been established for the particular benefit of the (*school or unit*) is deemed a part of the University of Texas (*institution*) Advisory Council and is subject to these Bylaws. Such internal foundations are to function as an accounting and administrative mechanism in the name of which the Council may approach prospective donors.[12] Internal foundations are not encouraged and shall not be established or maintained except with the approval of the president of the institution, the Vice Chancellor for External Relations, the appropriate Executive Vice Chancellor, the Chancellor, and the Board of Regents.[13]

Article X Amendments

These Bylaws may be amended at any regular meeting by vote of a majority of the members of the Council; provided the notice of such meeting states that amendment of the Bylaws is to be considered. However, all Bylaws are subject to, and must be consistent with, the Regents' *Rules*, U.T. System policies and the policies of the University of Texas (*institution*).

Article XI General Rules and Procedures

Subject to the Regents' *Rules* and other applicable University policies, if questions of procedure and organization that are not specifically covered herein are raised in connection with these Bylaws, then the current edition of *Robert's Rules of Order* or its successor publication, if any, shall control.

Source: University of Texas System, *http://www.utsystem.edu/ogc/general/modelpolicies.htm* (accessed March 8, 2007).

---

12 Regents' *Rules*, Series 60302, Section 6. The phrase "accounting and administrative mechanism" is taken from the prior version of the Regents' *Rules*, Part One, Chapter VII, 7.1.

13 Regents' *Rules*, Series 60302, Section 6.

EXAMPLE #3

THE WHITTIER COLLEGE POET COUNCIL
MEMBERSHIP DESCRIPTION

Purpose

Council members will serve as advisors to the president and to other senior officers during biannual meetings focused on an issue of pressing concern to the college.

Appointments and Term of Service

Members will be appointed for a two-year term and may be re-invited for an additional two-year term. Members will be invited to serve by the president, with input from the senior administration, particularly advancement, and the current members of the Poet Council.

Meeting Schedule

The Poet Council will meet twice a year, once in the fall and once in the spring. Meetings generally will be held on campus, but occasionally may be held in another city. Typically, meetings will be an evening and a full day and, whenever possible, will coincide with another major campus event.

Expectations of Council Members

Council members are expected to attend all meetings.

The role of Poet Council members is to provide a needed, fresh perspective on a particular issue; it is not to do the work of investigation or implementation. Reading material will be mailed prior to the meeting to prepare members for the discussion.

Council members are asked to assume the costs of travel to the meetings and accommodations, as needed.

It is hoped that Council members will demonstrate their commitment to Whittier's future by making the College a top priority in their philanthropic plans. Each year all Council members are expected to make a contribution to the Whittier Fund.

Agenda for the Meeting

At each meeting, one theme will be selected for in-depth discussion. The selection will be determined by the needs of college officers (i.e., based on planning underway at the college or an impending major change).

The meeting usually will begin with a short briefing by the college officer responsible for implementing policy in the area under examination, followed by questions and discussion both with the officer in attendance and separately. Meetings may include small group discussions, interaction with faculty and students, and, as relevant, tours of facilities. At the end of the day, Council members will have a debriefing session with the president. This meeting will be preceded or followed by a reception and dinner, hosted by the president or a member of her senior staff.

Staff Support

As a presidential initiative, the Poet Council will receive administrative support from the Office of the President.

Source: Whittier College, Office of the President, personal communication with author, February 16, 2007.

Cases

CASE #1

WHITTIER COLLEGE
Poet Council
(Independent, liberal arts college)

WHITTIER COLLEGE IS A FOUR-YEAR independent, residential, liberal arts college, located in Whittier, Calif. It traces its roots to the founding of the town by the Religious Society of Friends in 1887 and is named for John Greenleaf Whittier, the prominent Quaker poet and leader of the abolitionist movement. The college is governed by a board of trustees.

The college's athletic mascot is a poet, and the presidential advisory council, established by President Sharon Herzberger in 2005, is known as the Poet Council. Council members serve as advisors to the president and to other senior officers on challenges and opportunities at the college.

Poet Council members are invited to serve by the president, who receives suggestions from senior members of the administration, including the advancement office, and current council members. They are invited for a two-year term and can be re-invited for one subsequent term. Members of the Poet Council are typically alumni, but the council is distinct from the college's alumni association. There are plans to create a parallel Poet Parents Council. An individual in the President's Office provides staff support for the council.

Poet Council members are selected to reflect a diversity of backgrounds and talents, people who will be good ambassadors for the college and bring expertise to bear in advising the president and other senior officers. The membership description makes clear that the role of Poet Council members is to provide a needed, fresh perspective on particular issues; it is not to do the work of investigation or implementation.

Council membership comes with some explicit expectations, outlined in the membership description. Council members are expected to attend all meetings, and they receive reading material prior to the meetings to prepare for discussion. Council members are asked to assume the costs of travel to the meetings and accommodations, as needed. Council members are also expected to make Whittier a top philanthropic priority and to contribute to the Whittier Fund (the college's annual fund), but no minimum amount is required.

The council meets twice a year, once in the fall and once in the spring. Meetings are usually on campus, but may occasionally be held in another city. The meetings are often held in connection with another campus event, such as homecoming. They begin with an evening dinner and introduce the issue to be considered in an approximately six-hour meeting the following day.

The meeting usually begins with a short briefing by the college officer responsible for implementing policy in the area under examination, followed by questions and discussion both with the officer in attendance and separately. Meetings include small group discussions, interaction with faculty and students, and, as relevant, tours of facilities. At the end of the day, council members have a debriefing session with the president.

Council meetings have produced recommendations that were implemented, thus having an impact on the college. For example, one recent meeting focused on the identity and image of the college in the marketplace and another on the question of how to better reach out to and engage alumni. Council members helped the college's communications professionals analyze the strengths and weaknesses of printed and electronic images in its alumni communications, which resulted in the development of new strategies and designs.

President Herzberger emphasizes the importance of follow-up with the council. A meeting summary is mailed after each meeting, and the council receives a report at the subsequent meeting on what changes were undertaken as a result of their recommendations.

Sources: Whittier College, Office of the President, personal communication with author, February 15, 2007; Whittier College Web site, *http://www.whittier.edu.*

CASE #2

THE GEORGE WASHINGTON UNIVERSITY
Leadership Retreat

(Independent research university)

THE GEORGE WASHINGTON UNIVERSITY is an independent research university, founded in 1821 and located in Washington, D.C. The university has nine major academic units, including the Columbian College of Arts and Sciences, the Elliott School of International Affairs, the Graduate School of Education and Human Development, the Law School, School of Business, School of Engineering and Applied Sciences, School of Medicine and Health Sciences, School of Public Health and Health Services, and College of Professional Studies.

The university's governing board is its board of trustees. Its alumni association is incorporated and interdependent with the institution. As an independent university, GW does not have a foundation for fundraising or the management of gift funds. There are advisory boards or councils associated with most of its nine academic units. The first was the National Council for Arts and Sciences, established in the early 1990s as an advisory group in the Columbian College of Arts and Sciences. Similar groups were subsequently created in other schools and have varied names—for example, the Law School Board of Advisors, the Business School Advisory Board, and the School of Engineering and Applied Science National Advisory Council. There are also advisory boards for the university's Virginia campus and for various specialized research and academic units. The activities of advisory boards and councils are managed by the advancement offices of the respective units, in coordination with their respective deans and the central university advancement office.

Members of school advisory councils held prominent leadership roles in the university's Centuries Campaign, which concluded in 2002, and a number have advanced to membership on the board of trustees. As the university prepared for another major campaign in 2006, its central advancement office worked with the unit-based advancement offices and the alumni relations staff to plan and conduct a program known as the 2006 GW Leadership Retreat. More than 250 members of the university's board of trustees, alumni associations, advisory boards and councils, and administration gathered for two days at a nearby off-campus site to discuss GW's progress toward goals, challenges facing the university and higher education, and the university's vision and plans for the future.

The program included social activities as well as speakers and smaller discussion groups. Discussions were led by the university's president, vice presidents, deans, and trustees on such topics as "Building Academic Infrastructure for Enhancing Our Research Capabilities," "Implications of Science and Technology for the 21st Century University," and "Securing Our Financial Future: The Role of Philanthropy."

The discussion groups were a mixture of trustees, university executives, and members of the various advisory councils to ensure the perspectives of each school and the overall institution were represented and provide participants with opportunities to meet others who share their involvement in the university. Some school advisory councils held separate meetings on the final day of the retreat to discuss their own unit's priorities in view of the overall university vision and plans.

GW's Vice President for University Advancement Laurel Price Jones, who held overall responsibility for planning and managing the program, described the 2006 Leadership Retreat as "a great occasion that allowed all the university's leadership to share perspectives on GW's future directions. It also helped to build camaraderie and teamwork among our multiple volunteer groups as we prepared to launch the largest campaign in our history."

Source: The George Washington University, personal communication with author, February 19, 2007.

CASE #3

UNIVERSITY OF MEMPHIS
Board of Visitors

(Public research university within system)

FOUNDED IN 1912 as West Tennessee State Normal School, the University of Memphis is today a public, metropolitan university enrolling more than 20,000 students in undergraduate, graduate, and professional degree programs. More than 850 faculty teach in ten colleges and schools and the university is home to five state-approved centers of excellence and the FedEx Institute of Technology. The University of Memphis is the research institution within the Tennessee Board of Regents System. The Board of Regents governs all public higher education institutions in the state that are not campuses of the University of Tennessee system.

The University of Memphis Board of Visitors was created in 1989, when a group of prominent Memphis business and community leaders came together to help advance the university, then known as Memphis State. The board worked to increase the university's national stature, enhance relationships with the local community, and assist in raising private funds. The board has been involved with past presidential searches and supported changing the institution's name in 1994 to the University of Memphis, to better reflect its regional and national mission and differentiate it within the system.

While the Board of Visitors has no formal bylaws, it follows guidelines that limit membership to no more than 40 members and that place limits on terms of service. Members are appointed by the president, who works with the board's nominating committee. The mayors of the city and county in which the university is located serve as ex-officio members and members of the system's Board of Regents from the Memphis area are also invited to participate. The Board of Visitors advises the president and helps the university with political, personal, and financial influence.

The University of Memphis Foundation, created in 1964, is an institutionally related foundation that accepts and manages private gifts to benefit the university. The foundation's board has fiduciary responsibility for funds managed by the foundation and operates under a formal charter and bylaws. Its members are elected by the foundation board itself according to its bylaws. The foundation board is thus legally distinct from the Board of Visitors. In 2003, the university observed that membership of the two boards included many of the same people and moved to a coordinated meeting format.

Meetings of the Board of Visitors and the foundation board occur sequentially on the same day, but with separate agendas and a different focus. The Board of Visitors discusses a topic or question facing the university and is strictly advisory to the president. Minutes are written and distributed, but no votes are taken. For example, at recent meetings the board discussed the implications of raising admission standards and how the broader community might perceive changes in academic programs.

The Board of Visitors' meeting adjourns and the group then reconvenes as the board of the University of Memphis Foundation, taking up the more formal business of managing the foundation's resources. Minutes are also written and record the board's formal actions concerning the foundation's business.

Asked for her advice on creating an advisory board, President Shirley C. Raines encourages presidents to seek broad representation of the community. Noting that having business people involved is important for fundraising and other reasons, she advises, "Having wider representation enables you to obtain a better understanding of how potential issues may be perceived by the broader community."

Sources: University of Memphis, personal communication with author, February 26, 2007; University of Memphis Web site, *http://www.memphis.edu.*

CASE #4

UNIVERSITY OF MARYLAND COLLEGE PARK
Robert H. Smith School of Business
Dean's Advisory Council and Board of Visitors
(Public university, professional school)

THE UNIVERSITY OF MARYLAND COLLEGE PARK is a public research university. As the flagship campus of the University of Maryland System, it enrolls over 35,000 undergraduate and graduate students with over 3,600 part-time and full-time faculty in 13 colleges and schools offering 127 undergraduate majors and 112 graduate degrees.

The Robert H. Smith School of Business is ranked among the top business schools in the nation. The school enrolls nearly 3,000 undergraduate business majors, 225 full-time MBA students, 970 part-time MBA students, and 106 Ph.D. students. More than 200 students are enrolled in Executive MBA programs worldwide.

The Dean of the Smith School, Howard Frank, is advised by two groups with distinct missions: the Dean's Advisory Council and the Board of Visitors. The University of Maryland College Park Foundation is an institutionally related foundation that serves the entire campus, including the business school. Some individuals on the Dean's Advisory Council and the Board of Visitors also serve on the foundation board, although no formal relationship exists between the two school-based groups and the foundation. There is also an alumni association chapter associated with the Smith School, which is distinct from the Dean's Advisory Council and the Board of Visitors.

The Dean's Advisory Council and the Board of Visitors each has 50 members appointed by the dean, who serve fixed, staggered terms. There are written guidelines on the terms of membership but not formal bylaws. Both groups meet twice per year, separately, and are managed by staff in the school's Office of External Relations, which employs 20 individuals. The staff, which includes a team of events management professionals, divide responsibility for the two groups' meetings, communications, and events. The Dean's Advisory Council has existed for many years and was strengthened five years ago, at the same time the Board of Visitors was created. The co-chairs of the advisory council serve on the Board of Visitors, but the membership is otherwise distinct.

Members of the Dean's Advisory Council are all alumni of the school and focus internally on activities to strengthen the school, including mentoring students, advising on curriculum, branding, and fundraising. It has provided leadership in several recent initiatives. For example, members raised funds to obtain a box at the university's athletic arena, which is used to cultivate friends and donors of the school. The council also initiated the annual Smith School Awards, and its members participate in the program by presenting the awards.

The Board of Visitors includes senior level corporate executives from across the nation and the world. Members serve by virtue of their corporate positions rather than alumni status, although some members are alumni. The board is externally focused, helping the school develop corporate partnerships and keeping faculty apprised of industry needs to inform their curricular offerings. While fundraising is not an explicit aspect of its mission, relationships developed through the board have resulted in new resources for the school.

Dean Frank acknowledges that having two groups, each meeting twice per year, requires a substantial investment of time and effort. In addition, he meets with members of both groups between meetings, frequently in small groups. He emphasizes the different missions and composition of the two groups, recognizing that combining them would create meetings that would be too large to facilitate discussion. He also notes the importance of having sufficient staff to support the council and board's activities and the benefit of combining their meetings with other campus events. For example, one meeting may be held on the same day as a meeting of the foundation board and another in conjunction with an athletic event. A meeting of the Dean's Advisory Council is held at the same time as the school's undergraduate awards banquet where some members serve as presenters. As the dean observes, combining meetings and events in this way provides a more efficient use of staff, because they are already involved with the other activities. The model also helps to build the commitment of members through their involvement in the life of the school and contact with students and faculty. As an example of how involvement builds relationships, Dean Frank cites one alumnus who reported that his Maryland diploma had once been displayed in his basement recreation room. As his involvement with the advisory council increased and his relationship with the school developed, the diploma was moved to the first floor family room and subsequently to the entry hallway of his home, where it is one of the first things visitors see.

Asked for his advice to other deans, Frank emphasizes having a clear purpose for the advisory group and keeping it focused on its mission, engaging the group in substance and not just show-and-tell, combining meetings with other activities to gain efficient use of members' time and that of the dean and staff, and committing sufficient staff and resources to manage the activities of the groups effectively. Is it worth the time and effort? Does it pay off? "Very definitely," he replies. "We do not require giving by members of either group, although some have been significant donors. But the value of their time and contacts, the assistance they provide to students and faculty, and the advice they provide to the dean are more valuable than any financial gifts they could make."

Sources: University of Maryland Robert H. Smith School of Business, personal communication with author, February 28, 2007; University of Maryland Robert H. Smith School of Business Web site, *http://www.rhsmith.umd.edu/.*

CASE #5

STETSON UNIVERSITY
College of Arts and Sciences Advisory Board
(College within an independent university)

STETSON UNIVERSITY WAS FOUNDED IN 1883 as Florida's first independent university and today enrolls more than 2,000 undergraduate students as well as students in master's degree programs and in a law school. Stetson's main campus near Daytona Beach and Orlando, Fla., is home to the College of Arts and Sciences, the School of Business Administration, and the School of Music. The College of Law is located in St. Petersburg/Gulfport, the Stetson University Center at Celebration is near Orlando, and a new downtown Tampa Law Center and campus opened in 2004. Stetson is governed by a board of trustees. The College of Arts and Sciences is Stetson's oldest and largest academic unit, offering more than 40 undergraduate majors and minors and graduate degree programs in English, counselor education, and teacher education. Grady W. Ballenger has been dean of the college since 1998.

The College of Arts and Sciences Advisory Board includes 24 individuals. The college also has separate advisory councils focused on teacher education and counselor education, and they play a role in the accreditation of their programs. Stetson's schools of music, business, and law also have advisory boards similar to the College of Arts and Sciences Advisory Board.

Members of the College of Arts and Sciences Advisory Board are nominated by the dean of the college and are appointed by the president with ultimate approval by the Board of Trustees. Under its bylaws, advisory board members serve three-year terms and must leave the board for at least one year after their second consecutive term before becoming eligible for reappointment to a third term. The board meets twice each year with staff support from the college's advancement office.

Dean Ballenger cites the advisory board's leadership in gaining approval and funding for a new science building as one of its significant recent accomplishments. The need for a science facility had been recognized for many years, especially by members of the advisory board. The board includes alumni who are faculty members at other institutions, physicians, corporate executives of science-oriented companies, and others who have a keen interest in science education. The chair of the advisory board serves ex-officio on the University's board of trustees. In addition, two previous chairs now hold membership on the board of trustees. The advisory board thus has served as a source of leadership for the overall university and has produced trustees who already have a good understanding of programs and needs at the college level. The current advisory board chair and advisory board alumni were principal advocates for the new science building. They persuaded the Board of Trustees not only to approve the project but also to pledge $7 million toward the first phase of construction.

The advisory board has also supported the college in other important ways. Members assist in recruiting students. Some have hosted small groups of prospective students in their homes, at which the dean or a faculty member speaks. Dean Ballenger says this personal approach and the endorsement of advisory board leaders makes a strong and positive impression on prospective students, which has encouraged some to attend Stetson. Advisory board members who are corporate executives also have helped students obtain internships and jobs.

Advisory board members are expected to make personal gifts, although no minimum amount is required. Dean Ballenger observes that involvement often leads to increased

73

interest and commitment, and some advisory board members have made personal gifts for purposes of particular interest to them, including scholarships and lecture series, among others. Some have made charitable provisions in their estate plans for significant gifts to benefit the college.

Asked for his advice to other deans who may be establishing or working with an advisory council, Dean Ballenger offers three points. First, be aware that developing relationships with the board is time-consuming. It requires not only the regular meetings but also continuing involvement between them. A dean planning to establish a board needs to commit sufficient time to the program and ensure the board receives sufficient staff support. Second, he says, "Choose the right people to serve, based on your goals for the board. Be sure you have a good understanding with the president and advancement staff about the role of the board and the types of individuals you are seeking as members." Finally, work closely with the board's chair in planning meeting agendas and the topics to be discussed. Avoid show-and-tell and engage them in substantive matters. Dean Ballenger cautions that curriculum can be a sensitive topic, as faculty have responsibility for these decisions. Nevertheless, it is possible to identify other subjects and issues on which the board's guidance will be appropriate and useful. For example, Stetson's advisory board discussions are often organized around themes such as diversity, undergraduate research, faculty development, and facilities.

Sources: Stetson University College of Arts and Sciences, personal communication with author, March 2, 2007; Stetson University Web site, *http://www.stetson.edu.*

Advice from the Trenches

PRESIDENTS AND DEANS RESPONDING to the 2006 AGB survey were asked what they would provide as "one short piece of advice" to others about working with or starting an advisory council. Their responses were varied and reflect some differences of opinion, as well as much wisdom and experience. Some have been cited throughout the book. Below are selected responses, in their own words, grouped under major topics to which they apply.

Value of Advisory Councils

- [An advisory council] is clearly a way to involve very important and helpful people in the important affairs of the university. You get very few drawbacks and a lot of great positives from a group such as this.

- The advisory board should be a proving ground for future members of your governing board. If they show a willingness to donate time and money on the advisory board, they are good candidates for the governing board.

- Be highly involved and fully committed to this concept. It can be a very powerful advancement tool if used properly; if not, the complete opposite.

- Advisory boards take a great deal of nurturing. The time put into advisory boards is greater than the benefit, unless they are used extensively for strategic planning.

- Individuals on the board are…helpful personally when there is a need or issue to be resolved.

Advisory Council Purposes and Role

- Clearly state the purpose of the group so that the group does not believe that they have management responsibilities.

- Be sure you spell out duties and length of service very carefully. Do not assume the group will be satisfied with what they are doing, as they often wish to expand their [range] of influence.

- Identify concrete tasks for the advisory council.

- Do a self-study of the council, and put in place a plan to make the council serve the needs of the institution.

- Make sure their purpose is clear, and don't ask for advice when you don't really want it.

- Have a clear focus about the purpose of the board if starting one. Difficult to shift the culture from an advisory board to a fund-raising board once it is established.
- Don't have them dealing with curricular or other internal faculty matters that are outside their expertise.
- Steer clear of curriculum issues.

Giving and Fundraising

- Make fund-raising a requirement.
- Expect leadership in the area of fund-raising.
- Focus on members' ability/willingness to make a financial commitment.
- I suggest you ask for money in some range from each member.
- When recruiting members, be clear about the scope of responsibilities especially the expectations for fund-raising or personal donations.
- Select members who are willing to devote time and some monetary support to the college programs.
- Do not create one unless it is absolutely clear that a board is the only way to obtain significantly more donations.
- Have clear expectations for membership that involves individual personal contributions, and bringing their corporations to the table.
- If they do not contribute financially, their heart is really not in it.
- Don't always have your hand out. If you do everything else right, that will come with time.
- It is important to segregate fund-raising from the role of an advisory board.

Advisory Council Organization and Management
Membership

- Be sure to pick the right people, or it will be an unending source of trouble.
- Pick people you trust and those who have you and the university as a major interest.
- Keep [the requirements for membership] flexible.
- Don't keep people on it more than a few years.
- Avoid putting people on the board [who] have significant conflict of interest potential.
- If advice is the goal, the group should be small enough (10 to 15) to facilitate real discussion. I have found that council members want to be involved in a significant way.
- Select first for passion and commitment.
- Get the right people on the "bus," and make what you do both meaningful to the council and the college.

- Try to pick members that will participate, regardless of others' recommendations. Listen to current members and their recommendations first.

- Ensure that there is good diversity on the board in several respects—age, gender, background, time, talents, and treasure.

- Grow membership gradually, and keep it at a workable size. Consider a separate "Friends of..." organization for more casual relationships.

- I would suggest from experience that it is likely better to start with a small group of committed members than to devote too much energy to convincing others to join.

- Be creative in developing advisory council members. Look for leaders 3–5 years out. Pick people who are committed to the institution yet willing to be objective and offer constructive criticism.

77

Leadership

- Give careful thought and analysis to the chair of the board.

- Appoint or elect a president or chair of the board as soon as the board is moderately cohesive, so the thrust of the activities are driven from the membership.

- The chair of the council makes a significant difference in determining its effectiveness.

- Have an advisory board chairperson that complements your leadership strengths and don't tell them what you want to hear.

Structure and Policies

- Have formal bylaws that provide for a rotation off the board if a member becomes inactive. It is very awkward to ask a long-time member who never participates to roll off the board.

- Limited terms with the opportunity to serve consecutive terms—it's a nice way to eliminate individuals from the council who are no longer interested or no longer able to participate.

- Reappoint and renew membership when you first take the job.

- Create an executive committee to vet new members before their appointment.

- Clearly define board's charter and specific role of board subcommittees.

- Establish bylaws, and make sure there are term limits on how long members can serve.

- Have clear and set term limits; e.g., three-year terms, with two terms max in sequence.

- An advisory council should exist to help the dean. If the dean feels it is not helpful, then the dean should change it so that it is helpful. We formerly had a set of bylaws, and it was very rigid—Robert's Rules of Order were observed and so on. I removed all of that and basically use the advisory council for advice and ideas, then we have lunch. It works well.

Staffing and Support

- Needs a responsible, well-organized staff member who can fit it into his or her responsibilities.

- Hire a good development director who manages most of the communication.

- Make sure there is someone in the dean's office who can play a significant role in organizing meetings and communications.

- Ensure that the university president and development VP support the board fully. Ensure that there is a development person assigned to the board.

Advisory Council Meetings and Activities

- Give them an issue to help decide at each meeting. Don't spend a lot of time talking TO them. Break the advisory group into small discussion groups and have them report out. Don't make the meetings longer than 2 1/2 hours including a reception.

- Do not consume the meetings with speeches from the president or others. Get the members involved in brainstorming or other activities in which their expertise can be accessed and valued.

- Provide opportunities for advisory board members to hear the voice of undergraduate students.

- Give them almost the same background information as you give the governing board, except for personnel information.

- Send the agenda prior to the meeting so they have time to think about their input. Let them do most of the talking at the meeting and have someone take notes on the advice they give. Report back on any actions taken as a result of advice given at a previous meeting.

- Bring the members in for one day to deal with a critical question you are grappling with—no homework, no follow-up work. Just pick the brains of some smart, caring "outsiders."

- If you want to have top leaders in their fields, don't plan [a meeting schedule that is] too ambitious. We find that one substantive meeting a year is better than more with minimal participation.

- Build enthusiasm at the beginning of each year by having a group of students make a presentation on projects they are performing using business skills, for example, business plan or finance plan competition teams.

- These folks want to work and want to contribute in meaningful ways to the college. They are not interested in busy work or dog-and-pony shows. They are very talented and contribute a can-do, "real-world" dimension to thinking about the college and higher education.

- For every 15 minutes of presentations by college people, let the board talk for 45 minutes…. They cannot give advice if the academics don't give them a chance to voice their opinion! Keep the meetings lively with a variety of topics in an 8-hour day.

- Keep your conversation focused on the long-run, rather than trivial short-run issues.

Continuing Involvement

- Keep them engaged. Communicate with them three times per year beyond the annual gathering. Seek their counsel and provide opportunity for them to give counsel.

- Be in constant communication with the board through e-mail and newsletters.

- Make sure that the members have some level of ownership in the council to get their active participation. Just having them come to meetings once or twice a year is wasting the opportunities for them to help your college all during the year.

- Look for ways to involve certain members beyond the annual meetings. In other words, have an ongoing agenda for some members that includes other meaningful opportunities for engagement.

- Newsletters/updates need to be sent between meetings when…meetings are [only] two times per year.

- Engage them in the school itself—as guest lecturers, curriculum development, etc.

Working with Your Advisory Council

- Be open. Be informal. Be candid.

- Be very open about the challenges that you face.

- Treat them well; spend more time listening than telling.

- Be open, honest, and thorough in communicating facts about the school.

- Treat the advisory board as if it is the board of trustees, and stay in constant contact.

- Get to know each member personally.

- Be a good listener, and act on good advice. Be prepared to say "Thanks, but that won't work," when that is the case.

- Honestly engage them. Seek their advice and use it, and then let them know you used it.

79

Index

A

Advancement or development offices
fundraising and, 53–54
role in identifying or selecting council members, 33–34
Advice to members of advisory boards and councils
be clear about the purpose of the council before accepting membership, 54–55
be prepared to make an appropriate financial commitment, 55
consider your motivations for serving, 55
continuing involvement, 79
expect your advice to be taken seriously, 56
fundraising and donations, 76
get to know the institution and its people, 56
insist on discussions of real questions and issues at meetings, 55–56
leadership issues, 77
meetings and activities, 78–79
organization and management issues, 76–77
from presidents and deans, 75–79
purposes and role of advisory councils, 75–76
remember your appropriate role, 55
staffing and support, 78
structure and policies, 77
take pride and satisfaction from your work, 56
think about what you add to the council, 55
value of advisory councils, 75
working with advisory councils, 79
Advisory boards and councils
benefits of membership, 15
"bifurcated board" concept, 16
case studies, 65–74
challenges of, vii–viii
chapter synopses, x
characteristics, 8–9
common names for, 9–10
compared with governing boards, vii
example of council mission statement: independent institution (exhibit), 27
example of council mission statement: public institution (exhibit), 27
example of council responsibilities: independent institution, law school (exhibit), 28
example of council responsibilities: independent institution, professional school (exhibit), 28
governance continuum, 10
increase in the number of, ix
increasing importance of, vii
overlapping membership with other boards and councils, 11–12
responsibilities, 8–9, 17, ix, vii
size issues, 16
value of, 18–27
Alumni association boards
overlapping membership with other boards and councils, 11–12
role and responsibilities, 8
Association of Governing Boards of Universities and Colleges
report on self-regulation by higher education, 4
2006 survey on the purposes, activities, and operations of advisory boards and councils, 12–14, ix
Axelrod, Nancy
liability issues for board members, 11
terminology for advisory groups, 10

B

Best practices
    assigning specific work, 52
    budget and staff support issues, 53–54
    communicating with members between
        meetings, 53
    defining a clear purpose for the council, 50,
        52, 75–76
    encouraging council members' involvement
        in other areas of the institution, 54
    establishing and communicating a clear
        structure, 50–51, 77
    fundraising, 52–53, 76
    giving feedback on advice offered, 53
    illustrating and dramatizing the council's
        contributions, 53
    membership selection, 51–52, 76
    respecting the council's commitment, 54, 56
Board of trustees. See Governing boards
Boards in higher education. See also specific
        types of boards
    accountability issues, 4
    challenges in finding members, 2–3
    competition for top students and financial
        resources, 3
    fundraising, 11–14
    give-or-get policies for board members, 3
    lay governance, 1–2
    need for external groups to support
        governing boards, 4–5
    overlapping membership in boards and
        councils, 11–12
    questions for presidents, chancellors, and
        deans, 14, 26
    relationships among an institution's boards
        and councils, 11–12
    roles of governing boards, 2–3
    types of boards and councils (table), 6
    "wealth" role, 2
    "wisdom" role, 2
    "work" role, 2
BoardSource
    materials on advisory groups, ix
Boise State University
    College of Social Sciences and Public Affairs
        Advisory Council committees, 36, 38

Bylaws, guidelines, and job descriptions
    bylaws description, 29–30
    do councils have bylaws and job descriptions?
        (table), 29
    informal versus formal, 50–51
    samples, 57–64

C

CASE. See Council for Aid to Education
Case studies
    George Washington University Leadership
        Retreat, 67–68
    Stetson University College of Arts and
        Sciences Advisory Board, 73–74
    University of Maryland College Park Robert
        H. Smith School of Business, 71–72
    University of Memphis Board of Visitors,
        69–70
    Whittier College Poet Council, 65–66
Chait, Richard P.
    challenges in finding board members, 2–3
Claremont Graduate University
    example of council responsibilities:
        independent institution, professional
        school (exhibit), 27
Columbia University Law School
    Board of Visitors committees, 36, 39
    example of council responsibilities:
        independent institution, law school
        (exhibit), 27
Committees
    costs of organizing, 39
    example of advisory council committees
        (private institution) (exhibit), 37
    example of advisory council standing
        committees (public institution)
        (exhibit), 38
    example of committees (private institution
        professional school) (exhibit), 39
    limiting the number of, 39
    role and responsibilities, 36–40, 51
Communication issues
    advice from presidents and deans, 79
    communication and involvement between
        council meetings, 47–48, 53
    establishing and communicating a clear
        structure, 50–51, 77

Costs and benefits
   advice to council members, 54–56
   best practices, 50–54
   risks, 47
   time commitment, 47
Council chairs
   advice from presidents and deans, 77
   appointment of, 51
   method for selecting advisory council chair
      of those who have a chair (table), 35
   role and responsibilities, 35
Council for Aid to Education
   board gifts as a percent of individual giving, 3
Council meetings
   advice from presidents and deans, 78–79
   advisory council meeting activities (table), 43
   attendance requirements, 51
   big picture, "long-run" issues and, 44
   communication and involvement between
      meetings, 47–48, 53
   curriculum or academic policy and, 44
   discussion of issues, priorities, and plans,
      43–44, 55–56
   examples of discussion topics, 44
   frequency of, 42, 51
   fundraising and prospects and, 44–46
   planned agendas for, 42, 52
   presentations, 43
   sensitive matters and, 43–44, 52
   "show-and-tell" activities, 43, 52, 55
   social events, 46
   typical meeting activities, 43
Curriculum
   advisory boards' and councils' input, 19–20
   council meetings and, 44

D

Davidson College
   Board of Visitors, 10
Deans. See also Presidents
   advice from the trenches, 75–79
   council member selection, 32, 34
   fundraising and, 45
   identification of advisory groups as "boards,"
      10
   need for advisory groups, 9

overlapping membership of boards and
      councils, 12
   size of advisory councils, 31
   value of advisory boards and councils, 18–26,
      49
   working with advisory boards and councils,
      41–48
Duke University Fuqua School of Business
   Board of Visitors, 19–20
Dunlop, David
   "Five-I's" of involvement in fundraising, 22–24

F

Faculty
   inclusion on councils, 32
   interaction of councils with, 46–47
   presentations at council meetings, 43
"Five-I's" of involvement in fundraising, 22–24
Foundation boards
   independent type, 7
   interdependent type, 7
   role and responsibilities, 7–8
Fundraising
   advancement or development offices and,
      53–54
   advice from presidents and deans, 76
   best practices, 52–53
   council identification of goals and objectives
      for a campaign, 45
   council meetings and, 44–46
   deans' role, 45
   "Five-I's" of involvement, 22–24
   liability issues, 11
   minimum gift policies, 24–25, 52–53
   sense of ownership and personal
      responsibility for, 23–24
   social events and, 23, 46
   summary of the council's own giving and,
      45–46

G

George Washington University Leadership
      Retreat
   case study, 67–68

example of bringing the volunteer leadership of a university together in the context of preparing for a campaign, 47

Georgetown University
Board of Regents, 10
overlapping membership of boards and councils, 11
President and Directors of Georgetown College, 10

Governing boards
alumni associations and, 8
compared with advisory councils, vii
joint events with the advisory council, 47
legal obligations, 25
need for external groups' support, 4–5
overlapping membership with other boards and councils, 11–12
role and responsibilities, 6–7
size issues, 31

Grassley, Sen. Charles
nonprofit accountability, 4

Guidelines. *See* Bylaws, guidelines, and job descriptions

H

Harvard University
Board of Overseers, 6, 10
Harvard Corporation, 6

Holland, Thomas P.
challenges in finding board members, 2–3

I

Independent institutions. *See* Private institutions

Ingram, Tom
brochure on advisory groups, ix
liability issues for board members, 11

Iowa State University
sample bylaws of the College of Liberal Arts and Sciences Dean's Advisory Council, 57–58

J

Job descriptions. *See* Bylaws, guidelines, and job descriptions

K

Klausner, Michael
"bifurcated board" concept, 16

L

Lay governance
advantages of, 1–2
members as institutions' largest donors, 1
needs and expectations of the business community and the public and, 1–2
protection of institutions from political and ideological pressures, 1

Legon, Richard
Margin of Excellence: The New Work of Higher Education Foundations, 7, 8

M

Margin of Excellence: The New Work of Higher Education Foundations (Legon), 7, 8

Marquette University
National Engineering Advisory Council committees, 36, 37

Membership issues
advancement or development office role in identifying or selecting council members, 33–34
advice to council members, 54–56, 75–79
alumni, 32
diversity of backgrounds, 51
faculty inclusion on councils, 32
groups frequently represented, 32
high standards for, 51–52
how council members are elected or appointed to serve (table), 33
large councils and, 52
multiple invitations and, 34–35
need to choose advisory council members with care, 34
number of members, 32, 51
selection, 33–35, 51–52

uncoordinated recruiting and, 35

who serves on advisory councils? (table), 32

Methodist University

Board of Visitors mission statement (exhibit), 18

Minimum gifts

arguments for and against, 24–25

giving in proportion to financial capacity, 25, 52–53

"money left on the table" argument, 25

policies on minimum annual gifts, 24

Motivations for service on advisory boards and councils

academic community participation, 16–17

benefits to individual members, 15–16, 52, 55

concern with governing responsibilities, 16

new experiences, 15–16

O

Operations and structure

advice from presidents and deans, 77

committees, 36–40

council chairs, 35

method for selecting advisory council chair of those who have a chair (table), 35

terms of service, 35–36

Organization and management issues

advice from presidents and deans, 76–77

bylaws, guidelines, and job descriptions, 29–30, 77

committees, 36–40, 51

constituencies represented, 32–33

council chairs, 35, 51

membership, 30–35, 76

operations and structure, 35–40, 77

questions for presidents, chancellors, and deans, 40

selection of members, 33–35, 51–52

size, 30–32

terms of service, 35–36, 51, 77

Ostrower, Francie

Why the Wealthy Give, 15

P

Presidents. *See also* Deans

advice from the trenches, 75–79

council membership, 32, 34

identification of advisory groups as "councils," 10

need for advisory groups, 9

overlapping membership of boards and councils, 12

size of advisory councils, 31

value of advisory boards and councils, 18–26, 49

working with advisory boards and councils, 41–48

Private institutions. *See also* Public institutions

board members as donors, 3

case studies, 65–68, 73–74

competition for top students, 3

example of advisory council committees (independent institution) (exhibit), 37

example of committees (independent institution, professional school) (exhibit), 39

example of council mission statement: independent institution (exhibit), 18

revenue sources, 1

Public institutions. *See also* Private institutions

advisory councils' involvement in higher education advocacy, 21

appointment of governing board members, 6, 7

board members as donors, 3

boards as sources of philanthropic support, 7

bylaws for advisory boards and councils, 30

case studies, 69–72

competition for appropriated funds, 3

example of advisory council standing committees (public institution) (exhibit), 38

example of council mission statement: public institution (exhibit), 27

foundation boards, 7–8

governing boards, 6–7

local advisory boards, 7

quasi-governing boards, 7

revenue sources, 1

states' establishment of to meet agricultural research needs, 2

Purposes and roles of advisory boards and
councils
advice from presidents and deans, 75–76
motivations of individual board and council
members, 15–17, 52, 55
value of advisory councils, 18–26

Q

Quasi-governing boards
liability issues, 11
role and responsibilities, 7, 10

S

Sarbanes-Oxley Act
accountability issues for higher education
institutions, 4, 16
Seymour, Harold J.
motivation for board membership, 15–16
Size issues
most common size, 30, 51
size of advisory councils (table), *31*
small *versus* large, 16, 31, 51–52
Small, Jonathan
"bifurcated board" concept, 16
Smith, G.T. "Buck"
"Five-I's" of involvement in fundraising, 22–24
Staff issues
advice from presidents and deans, 78
best practices, 53–54
staff sources, 41
Stetson University College of Arts and Sciences
Advisory Board
case study, 73–74
Streetman, Ben D.
advisory council size, 31
Students
interaction of advisory councils with, 47, 56

T

Taylor, Barbara F.
challenges in finding board members, 2–3
Terms of service
"country club boards," 36
limits on, 35–36, 51

Tuck School of Dartmouth University
Board of Overseers, 10
2006 AGB survey
description, ix
key findings, 12–14

U

University of California
Board of Regents, 7, 10
University of Maryland College Park Robert H.
Smith School of Business
Dean's advisory council and Board of Visitors
case study, 71–72
University of Memphis Board of Visitors
case study, 69–70
University of Michigan
alumni association, 8
University of Texas at Austin
Engineering Advisory Board, 31
example of council mission statement: public
institution (exhibit), 27
University of Texas System
bylaws model, 30, 59–62
University of Virginia
Board of Visitors, 10

V

Value of advisory boards and councils
accreditation process, 20
administrative operations, 20
advice from presidents and deans, 75
advice sources, 19–20
"ambassador" role, 20–21
candidacy of members to assume greater
responsibility, 19
councils as "farm clubs," 18–19
curriculum issues and, 19–20
faculty recruitment, 21
fundraising, 22–24
higher education advocacy, 21
internal advocacy, 21
nonfinancial resources, 21
response of presidents and deans on the value
of advisory boards and councils, *18*
"speaker's bureau" source, 21

statements of purposes of, 25–26
strategic planning, 20
Voluntary Support of Education survey
financial support for public institutions, 3

W

Wartburg College
overlapping membership of boards and
councils, 11–12
Whittier College Poet Council
bylaws, 30, 63–64
case study, 65–66
Why the Wealthy Give (Ostrower), 15
Williams College
alumni association, 8
Working with advisory boards and councils
advice from presidents and deans, 79
budgetary support, 41–42, 53–54
communication and involvement between
meetings, 47–48
council meetings, 42–46, 51, 78–79
interacting with students and faculty, 46–47,
56
joint events with the governing board, 47
questions for presidents, chancellors, and
deans, 48
staff support, 41, 53–54

Y

Yale University
alumni association, 8

About the Author

MICHAEL J. WORTH IS PROFESSOR OF NONPROFIT MANAGEMENT in the School of Public Policy and Public Administration at the George Washington University in Washington, D.C., a position he has held since 2001. He teaches graduate courses related to the management of nonprofit organizations, nonprofit governance and board management, nonprofit enterprise, and fundraising and philanthropy. He is a consultant to educational institutions and nonprofit organizations in the areas of fundraising, strategic planning, board development, and general management issues.

Worth has more than 30 years of experience in philanthropic resource development, having served for 18 years as vice president for development and alumni affairs at George Washington and previously as director of development at the University of Maryland at College Park.

Worth has been a frequent speaker at conferences of the Council for Advancement and Support of Education (CASE), the Association of Fundraising Professionals, and the Association of Governing Boards of Universities and Colleges. He has conducted on-campus presentations and workshops for boards of trustees, presidents, deans, and advancement staff at colleges and universities across the country and abroad.

In addition to publishing numerous articles, reviews, and conference papers, Worth has written or edited five books, including *Securing the Future: A Fund-Raising Guide for Boards of Independent Colleges and Universities* (AGB 2005), which received the CASE 2006 Warwick Award for Outstanding Published Scholarship.

Worth has served as a member of CASE's Commission on Philanthropy and as editor of the *CASE International Journal of Educational Advancement*, a scholarly journal related to the fields of alumni relations, communications, and philanthropy. He advised CASE as special consultant for executive education in developing programs for senior advancement professionals and campus chief executives and has served as a faculty member at the Harvard Institutes for Higher Education.

He holds a B.A. in economics from Wilkes College, an M.A. in economics from American University, and a Ph.D. in higher education from the University of Maryland.